C000176676

Persua Skills

BLACK BOOK

of

Job Hunting Techniques

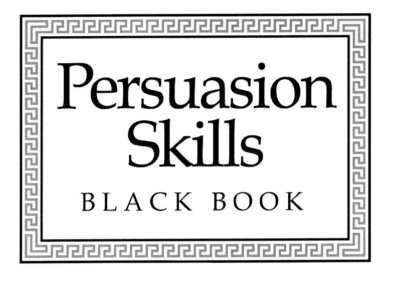

Persuasion Skills

BLACK BOOK

of

Job Hunting Techniques

Rintu Basu

First Published in Great Britain 2011
by www.BookShaker.com

Typeset in Book Antiqua

Contents

Praise

Praise for the system

The system in the *Persuasion Skills Black Book* has been developed over the last fifteen years and hundreds of people have been coached and trained to use it. In 2009 a download version of the system was created and the book is built from that experience. Here is some of the praise for the system:

The interview techniques helped me land a great job. It was so easy to apply these valuable tools. Even though I found the job of my dreams, I've gained the confidence I never had before and I just interviewed and got a position that I never even thought I could obtain.

Lake Mcalester, Engineer Manager, Houston Tx

I have found your job hunting info to be of great value as it has given me the confidence to go out and talk with anyone and show them the value that I have to offer. Instead of being on the backfoot I have been able to take the position of being the prize and getting them to want me as I do not have to fear the situation knowing that I am coming from a position of strength and knowing the right questions to ask and how to deflect their questions to me in an artful manner.

Robert Mokos

I was new to NLP when I decided to purchase NLP CV and Interview Skills and I have to say it did the job! I had been unemployed for about two months and struggling with re-writing my CV and projecting myself at interviews. Between using my usual sources I devoted time to the course and started to use it to change my CV and interview techniques. Miracles do happen! After about three weeks I found a position using the skills I was able to develop (it was my first interview using NLP techniques). For me, it was an excellent investment and continue to use it for different situations. I have recommended it to my family and friends.

Eric Brockhurst, Sales Manager, North London

I knew redundancy was on the cards within the next 6 months so I purchased an electronic copy "interview skills and CV techniques". I applied for voluntary redundancy and on the same day I applied for another job. I had an interview two days later. I got a call the next day from the agency, I wasn't very hopeful at such a quick response, however they had called to offer me the job. They decided to cancel the rest of the interviews as I was the right person. So I collected my redundancy money and walked straight into another job.

Paul Ross

The exhilarating realisation that you can take control of the interview with some of these techniques gives one an extremely effective competitive advantage.

Christopher

Worth every penny! I've bought many books about how to answer difficult interview questions and preparing for interviews and they all failed to deliver. After struggling with interviews I decided to get your interview pack as I always knew I can do the job but failed to get past the interview stage.

I remember using your system for my current job and wow the results were amazing, I kept on banging on about being able to deliver fantastic results and giving examples and towards the end of the interview I could feel the interviewer begging me to take the job as he said "Will are you still interested in the job?" and mentioning how he would see me fit in his organisation.

To cut a long story short the next day I received a call with a job offer and if I could start next week.

Will Tate, Accountant, Newcastle Upon Tyne

...other changes come from me being approached by companies to hire me instead of me having to conduct a multi-month job search. I hadn't gotten these kind of results before using the system. I've also used the system for business proposals so it applies across multiple mediums.

Matt Detrick, CHt "The Remarkable Hypnotist"

Explains the REAL reason a candidate is chosen, and gives you easy to follow strategies to REALLY make the difference. In such a competitive environment it made all the difference for me. I got the job!"

Barry, Sales Manager

Praise for this book

Rintu Basu is a brilliant persuader who has achieved worldwide acclaim by both using and teaching powerful influence techniques. His work is particularly outstanding because in addition to demonstrating techniques through his writing, he also explains them clearly and explicitly, so the reader can incorporate them in his life as well.

We receive dozens of job applicants per day, and the ones who excel in our interview process understand the ideas in Rintu's books.

Tadd Rosenfeld, Chief Executive Officer, TeamLauncher.com (also Chief Executive Officer, MarketingVentureCapital.com)

I used the Persuasion Skills Black Book of Job Hunting Techniques and re/designed my CV in accordance with the recommendations in the book. Within days of sending out the new revised CV I received three interview offers for the middle of September in August. I am now going to be focusing on my interview techniques and sending out a whole load more CV's.

Geraint

Wow. Human resources management may have met its match! This book could change the "hiring process" as we know it. Hiring managers won't stand a chance against these job hunting techniques. Now you can stand out among other candidates and get the edge in this competitive job market.

Joseph A. Alcala, HRM, NLP

The Persuasion Skills Black Book of Job Hunting Techniques provides great strategies for designing a CV to secure an interview and controlling the interview process to get a job offer. For anyone looking for a new job, read this book first for a much better chance of success.

David

I'm often asked by friends and relatives for my support in job applications, interview techniques etc. and I will definitely recommend the system (and of course the book!) to them to provide a systematic way to approach the daunting prospect of job hunting - the case studies are an excellent way to demonstrate the various tools and give confidence to the most timid of candidates.

Katie Bell, HR Executive

I am currently in the Military and will soon be hitting the job market. However my wife is now enjoying the rigors of seeking employment. She has been able to control the interview for the first time, and uses questions such as, "If I were doing a good job what do you see me accomplishing?" to draw mental pictures and direct the interviewer's thought process. She is now choosing which job she wants. From my wife and myself, Thank you!

Kevin Waters

Rintu highlights effectively the most important components to consider when seeking a change in jobs or when securing a new one.

Rintu has created a system that allows the reader to confidently shift perspective, taking the perceived pressure off job hunting, cv/application submission and those all-important interviews. I utilised the chapters on 'A winning attitude' and 'the first 2 minutes' at a recent interview with absolute ease using the system!

LR, London, Legal Administrator

This book is not one of the normal day to day run of the mill books on writing a CV or getting a job, it covers a wide range of subjects (NLP & Hypnosis) that will not only improve your CV writing skills and improve your knowledge of what an employer requires and wants it will help get you through the front door.

Being an ex-manager in local government, one of the most arduous jobs was sifting through 100's of prospective employees' CVs to narrow them down to how many I could be short listed to interview over three days. I can't put it strongly enough that CVs are the most important part of getting to the first stage on the Job ladder and the advice that come within the first 60 pages is worth the price alone. The chapters on CV construction are excellent highlighting your attributes and putting them on the first page is excellent advice, the advice in the following chapters make writing a CV a piece of cake!

This book is a must for anyone (young or old) applying for promotion or your first job.

John Gill, DIM

Within a week of reading your book I aced three interviews in a row. Ultimately I chose to work for a company who actually created a position for me after initially telling me they had no openings. Your techniques work like magic!

Shawn C

There is so much useful material here that I will go through the whole book again and again. This is not an extension of the Persuasion Skills Black Book, it's a completely separate entity designed specifically for preparing the best possible CV and interview. Brilliant stuff!

Gary

Having worked in HR for 15 years and conducted many interviews, I wasn't sure I would learn anything new. I was wrong! I especially loved the NLP techniques. As an NLP practitioner it was really useful to be reminded about the very powerful influence NLP techniques can have. I will most certainly be using them in my pursuit for a new job. The CV and the rationale provided by Rintu was spot on. I have now re-drafted my CV and sent it out to a couple of recruitment agencies.

Jane, Senior HR Practitioner

I enjoyed this book immensely; I was able to take tips and techniques about preparing my resume and immediately updated it. The sections on hypnotic answers present NLP based technique very well since the focus is narrow even a beginner will be able to use them and his expertise in interviewing on both sides of the table is shown many times over.

While I know looking for a new job, in this market it is already difficult, I believe information technology is one of the more dynamic ones and with this change comes the opportunity for advancement!

With Rintu's excellent book I know I have an edge few other applicants will even know about and I am excited that Rintu has provided such timely information.

Kenneth Hunt, IS Analyst, KennethHunt.com

The uniqueness about this book is that it contains latest psychological tools which lead towards the result. I recommend this and I suggest every jobseeker must grab this amazing guide.

Mayur Bardolia

I now have the confidence to apply for posts that a few weeks ago I considered beyond me. I am optimistic and confident now about the future.

Mike

Tried and true. A goal oriented approach on presenting yourself in the best possible way.

Joost Ploegmakers

The material makes excellent use of NLP modelling and language processes to allow the job seeker to level the playing field during the interview and make it into a truly two-way process. Clear, practical, and empowering ideas and exercises are provided for developing the right attitude, elegantly reframing objections, and nailing those difficult questions. This material is a core part of our client training.

Scott Byiers, Manager, Sair Centre of Learning,
www.saircentre.synthasite.com

The game has changed - this is how you win!

Tom Hinchey, Office Manager, London

This book was simply amazing! I never knew you could apply so much nlp/hypnosis to a job interview from start to end. Hands down, I must say that this book was the best on this particular topic that I've ever read. The best part is that it's so easy to read and actually implement. Your approach to teaching this material is exceptional.

I had a lot of fun reading this book, it felt as though Rintu was directly coaching me, as a conversation. I could feel the wealth of research, knowledge as well as effort that has been put into this book. I feel empowered after having completed the book.

I went out and used some of these principles in an interview; I didn't want the job but just wanted to try out the techniques. Needless to say I was offered the job and the best part was that I had so much fun giving the interview.

Bilal Rasool

This book is invaluable! I overhauled my resume in one evening from a list of tasks to a page of standout achievements and I learned how to get potential recruiters hooked in to find out how I had achieved my accomplishments. With this alone I was able to increase my number of interviews by 50%.

I learned how to use my resume as the building block for conducting an interview and actually taking the reins during the interview. This I admit was the most difficult part for me to grasp, but I am amazed how an adjustment in my attitude before the interview created such a powerful outcome.

I am now negotiating between three offers and it seems surreal.
Thank you!

Raymond G

Acknowledgements

S ome of the usual suspects appear for their unwavering support in helping me get this book off the ground. Just because you are constantly supportive, I hope I never take any of you for granted.

Whendie, without you, the work you have done with your clients, the discussions and support you have given me over the years, this book could not have been written. I am one of the growing number that see the great contributions you make to people's lives.

Sharon, Dave, John, you know who you really are; thanks for letting me tell your stories and illustrate the examples. Without your astounding successes in the job hunt there would have been no book to write.

Dave, thank you for your technical wizardry. I suspect this book would have been faster without the long lunches, practicing patterns and visits to the cinema, but I would choose fun over speed any day – long may it continue.

Mum and Dad, you were excited about a book even when you didn't know what it was going to be about.

Joe Gregory, my publisher, you have been a constant source of inspiration, ideas and support. Your experience has helped my writing to reach an audience. We must meet in person sometime.

The numerous people who bought the original system, your feedback, success stories and support have given me the inspiration to write this book.

The NLP Community, some of whom I have never

met, have made this book possible. Richard Bandler and John Grinder who started this NLP thing; David Shephard, my original NLP trainer; Mina McGuigan and NLP 96 have kept the spirit of NLP alive in Glasgow since 1996. Without you this book could not have even been conceived.

And finally all the recruiters, companies and organisations who have allowed me to research, test and play from both sides of the fence. Without you guys I could not have come up with this system. I hope it pays you back by getting you people who can really do you a service.

Foreword

I have seen Rintu transform the lives of many people, including my own. I first met Rintu in 2005 when he taught me the secrets of NLP and how to make it work for myself and others. It had a profound effect on my life and for that I am truly indebted to him. It helped me to visualise the future I wanted and increased my belief that I could achieve it with the help of others. Since meeting Rintu, I have focused on giving more, and I've received tenfold in return.

I was honoured when Rintu asked me to write the Foreword for this book. He recognises that, as a Talent Expert, I have significant experience in the key characteristics of high performers. When coaching high potential individuals I often refer to similar techniques to those mentioned in this book and applying these techniques will, in my opinion, clearly help you to excel in the skill of job hunting. The more you practise them, the luckier you will become.

Despite the depth of his examples, Rintu's book is easy to read and so many of his techniques are straight forward and easy to put into practice. In fact, whilst this book contains excellent guidance for job hunters, many of the tips have use in the wider aspects of life; I'm pleased to say that I learned a couple of new things myself. There are so many great suggestions within this book that even the most seasoned interviewee will learn something that will help them when going for future jobs.

I often recommend Rintu to others when I know his wisdom and methods are the key to unlocking their potential and I love the ideas in this book so much that I am already recommending this book to clients whom I am currently coaching. For example, remember. "The job hunting process isn't about you, it's about the client and their needs".

I wish them and you happy hours of reading and much success in applying the "secrets of the system".

Fraser Murray
Talent Expert with Rock The Boat Consulting, a global provider of Leadership Training, Talent Development and Executive Coaching www.rocktheboatconsulting.com/fraser-murray.html

Preface

My wish is that you can become completely free and let go of the shackles of employment. Over the years I've met many people who feel trapped in the rat race and in jobs that they don't enjoy. I find it amazing that people spend five out of their seven days a week in jobs that they profess to hate.

When you've taken away the number of hours that you spend sleeping, eating and doing chores, you spend more time working than doing anything else. Assuming you don't work with them, you spend more time doing your job than you spend with your loved ones, or investing in your hobbies and interests. I can't imagine how horrible life must be for those doing a job they dislike. I think you have a responsibility to yourself, to the people you are close to and the world in general to get a job that rewards and fulfils you.

I am very excited because I have seen the impact that gaining the skills in this book have had on many people. Imagine what it is like for someone who has felt constrained by their circumstances and suddenly finds themselves being able to choose. While they once thought they had to stay in their job, however much they felt undervalued and mistreated, they become able to pick and chose where they want to work and what they want to do. It is a hugely liberating feeling and I have watched from the sidelines as people have gone through that transformation. I hope this book brings you that gift.

I have other reasons for writing this book. I have

been on the other side of the fence; I have interviewed and employed people. Many times I have sat there thinking I would pay double for some people who had a spark, some enthusiasm or a desire to do the job.

With the skills you will gain from this book you will have no excuses. With these skills comes the right to have a great job, the responsibility to hunt those jobs out and give a great return on the investment of those employers fortunate enough to recognise your value.

Bonus Material

Dear Reader,

I want you to succeed. The book you are holding is the distillation of over fifteen years of work and I want to be as certain as possible that it will work for you as it has for the hundreds of people who have already been through the Job Hunting System.

To this end I have put together a couple of unique bonuses that you can use to help you get the job that you deserve.

Firstly, there is the CV template that we discuss in this book. You can download this as a Word document from my website completely free. All you need to do is fill in your details as explained later in the book and your hypnotically persuasive CV/résumé will be ready to work for you.

Secondly, you can download a free report that details over 500 interview questions including the most commonly asked and the most difficult to answer. When you learn the hypnotic answer formula later in this book you can test yourself against these questions and notice just how easy they are to answer.

To get these bonus downloads just go to
www.nlpinterviewtechniques.com/6319/bookbonus
and follow the onscreen instructions.

CV/Résumé Writing and Interview Skills

Why should you read this book?

Applying the system in this book will dramatically increase your chances of getting any job that you apply for. Will you get every job you apply for? No, there are too many variables to be able to guarantee that. But if you apply the system every time, you have a greater chance of success and you will eventually get what you want. With some perseverance and the methodology from this book you will get the job you are looking for.

Over the years that I have been training people in this methodology I have noticed that something interesting happen to the people that really take it on board. They become liberated from the ratrace and daily grind of their jobs. Consider this: if you knew you could go out and get a new job any time you wanted, how would your view of the world change?

I have noticed people using this system become more self-confident, happier and more satisfied at work. Think about it for a moment: if the only reason you were at your place of work was because you wanted to be there, wouldn't you make more of your job?

Here are some of the incredible successes I have been privileged to have witnessed firsthand:

Sharon, by applying the system twice in less than a

year, went from a problematic and hated job to doubling her salary and working in an international management role that she loves.

Frank making a complete career change from insurance salesman to storyboard artist with no art experience except for the fact he like to draw and had a portfolio.

Dave going for a job where he was four years younger than the average employee, had no experience and was up against heavy competition in a traditional, risk adverse industry.

Trevor, long-term unemployed, going for a management role and being offered the job even before he had managed to walk into the interview.

Maybe less dramatically, I have seen senior managers who were constantly passed over for promotion, get back on the career ladder. I have seen mothers returning to work after a career break to better jobs than they had left. I have seen ex-convicts land good jobs even after a prison sentence.

In all these cases the common denominator has been they have all applied the system. Not all results are the same and you may not get exactly the same outcomes as the people mentioned above. What I can say is that, as was the case for all of them, applying the system will get you better results than not applying the system. Taking these ideas to heart will change you from a wage slave to being in total charge of your career.

Where did the system come from?

Fifteen years ago I was privileged to be working with a team that was investigating interview techniques. We were looking for what worked and what didn't. I wanted to find out what worked in a live environment so I set about applying for all sorts of jobs using fake CVs (please note: this was research, not job hunting. In a job hunting scenario I suggest you always present the *truth* in the best possible light. Anything else is criminal).

I quickly found out what worked for CVs and in interview.

On one memorable occasion I was offered a £60,000 job after I had told them I had lied on the CV (they caught me out on the technical aspects of the job) and I did not have any of the relevant experience or qualifications they asked for. That is how powerful this system, properly applied, can be.

I personally have sat in over 100 interviews for a huge variety of roles at many different levels, trying out all the techniques I share in this book. I have also sat on the other side of the fence and have recruited hundreds of people from directors to front line staff in many different occupations. Over the last ten years I have personally coached hundreds of people into successfully getting their dream job.

It is not just about knowing what to do; I've used the system, shared it with others and distilled it into what is now this book. Properly applied, this system will sky rocket your career prospects. I know because I have seen just that happen to many people. I have also met people who have taken the information and done nothing with it. Ultimately the choice is yours. If you can make a commitment to reading this book, then make a commitment to develop the skills, otherwise what is the point?

A brief word about NLP, conversational hypnosis and covert persuasion skills

The techniques in this book incorporate the leading edge thinking from applied psychology, NLP, conversational hypnosis and covert persuasion skills. We will not overtly discuss these theories unless relevant. This book is about getting you the job you want. If you want to find out more about the ideas, techniques and concepts behind this book feel free to visit my website, Facebook page or have a look in *The Persuasion Skills Black Book*.

If you are reading this book to find out how to apply NLP, hypnosis and covert persuasion skills in a given context, it will for the most part be up to you to join the dots. You are always welcome, however, to contact me directly via my website or my Facebook page and I will be happy to help. Do not expect this book to discuss in depth theories about how these particular technologies can be applied to job seeking skills. Do expect specific how to techniques, applied to CVs, résumés and interviews.

For more ideas about how NLP, hypnosis and persuasion skills can be applied, feel free to have a look at:

The article page on my website:
www.theNLPcompany.com/techniques

and/or

The Facebook Persuasion Skills Page:
www.fbook.me/persuasion

Who Is This Book For?

This book is for a specific type of person. If you are unsure of what sort of job to apply for or need help in trying to shape your career, this is not the book for you. If you want answers to profound questions about your life and career, this book is not for you.

If, on the other hand, you are the sort of person who knows what kind of job you want and has the ambition to go get it, this book will help. But before we start, let me add a few caveats. Doing the things that are outlined in this book **will not** guarantee you a particular job in any specific company. Doing the things outlined in this book **will** guarantee that you stand a better chance of getting the job you want.

If you are 16 years old working in your local burger bar and you have ambitions to be the next CEO of Coca-Cola, don't expect this book to get you there in one step. It will, however, allow you to get successively better positions. So if you are 16 years old and you want to become the CEO of Coca-Cola this book will give you strategies that will allow you to get better and better jobs until you have gained the experience you need to allow you to become CEO.

Getting the job of your dreams is going to take more than just reading this book. You will need to do the exercises and have some courage when it comes to the interview and any job selection tests. I don't want to suggest that everything that I ask you to do in this book is easy. Sometimes it's going to take a little bit of courage and the ability to stand your ground as well as accepting nothing but the best from yourself.

In short, if you have an idea of the job that you want to go for and some relevant experience, this book has all sorts of ideas, tips and techniques that will give you the edge over the usual job seeking community. You might also note that relevant experience is not necessarily having done the job before, but more on that later.

The best thing about the ideas in this book is that once you have integrated the concepts you can keep repeating them over and over again. One of the stories that we will return to is about a woman I will call Sharon.

When I first met Sharon she was working as a trainer in a large organisation. She was having trouble with her manager, felt she could contribute far more than she was being allowed to and felt trapped. She had applied for several jobs both internally and with other companies and had been knocked back, not even getting to the interview stage.

After she had worked with me and rearranged her CV, Sharon applied for several training manager roles. She went to interview and got the first. She stayed in that job for six months and decided that she could do better still. She did another round of job seeking and got herself a very powerful training manager position. She had gone from a standard training position to doubling her salary and into a powerful international management role. Sharon achieved this in less than a year, albeit she had to change roles twice to get the job. That is how powerful this system is.

All of the ideas concepts and tips that Sharon used are laid out in this book. So if you are the sort of person who knows the job that you want and is prepared to do the work to get it, this book will give you a blueprint of how you can get that dream job quickly.

How To Use This Book

This book is a system. It starts from developing the right mindset and attitude which will take you all the way through to the end of the interview. The power in this approach is through using the whole system. If you have an interview tomorrow then please just jump to the interview sections, have a read through and do the exercises. If you apply this it will give you an edge, but if you have the time then use the whole system because it can be amazingly powerful.

If you like to flick through books picking out bits and pieces, feel free to do this. The book is designed for you to scan through and find the bits that you're most interested in. But also remember that the power of this approach is through applying the whole system.

You might want to recognise that the sexy bits of this book – for example how to handle objections, create hypnotically compelling answers and put your interviewers under pressure – are not the bits that get you the job. You will get the job through applying the whole system. Having the right attitude and mindset is every bit as important. If I were to pick one element above all else that makes the biggest difference it would be the first two minutes of the interview.

The majority of this book has been laid out in the same way as I would approach the subject if you were sitting in front of me. As much as possible I have applied the same hypnotic language patterns, processes and concepts to motivate you as I would expect you to use on your CV/résumé and in your interviews. This might mean that in some places my phraseology appears a bit strange; this will be for one of three reasons:

- I got it wrong – in which case let it go, there are more important things to worry about

- It is the way I speak normally – in which case let it go, we all have colloquialisms and I deliberately practise these so I can hide my hypnotic language patterns better

- I am deliberately structuring my language in a particular way to motivate you to improve your chance of getting the job you want – in which case let it go, you do want a better job don't you?

In most cases, if you are struggling with the meaning of a sentence or two imagine having someone say the words out loud to you. Just change the emphasis to different words until the meaning comes through. Then again, you could just read on, as the detail is not as important as the overall concept.

Local, industry and cultural bias

My experience is from the UK and therefore this is where most of these techniques have been worked out for. Over the fifteen years I have been coaching and training people in getting the job of their dreams, I have worked with many people from other areas of the world. These techniques work in every country, every industry and with every role. But you do need to apply common sense and fit into any biases, accepted norms for your particular circumstances. Let me give you a couple of examples.

I use the term CV (short for curriculum vitae) because that is the accepted phrase in the UK. Americans will be more used to the term résumé. But for our purposes they are the same thing and written in a very similar fashion.

You may find on the internet different definitions and templates for these things, but our reality will be that, apart from tweaks, the documents are the same. When you log onto the website for the bonuses that come with this book you will be able to download a CV/résumé template in which all you will need to do is fill in your details and it is ready to go.

Here is a more specific example of this sort of tweak. Mary was applying for a marketing position with a company that was very soft, new age and feminine in their approach. She put pastel pink, floral motifs on the borders of her CV. This is something I would strongly discourage for most CVs. Mary got the job and she also found out that the interviewers had been drawn to her CV specifically because of these motifs. In Mary's industry this was a good approach.

I am writing a book to reach as many people as possible. That means you will have to apply common sense and tweak the system to apply to your context.

Some dangers

Much is said about people lying to get jobs. In the UK and, I suspect, most other areas of the world, this would be classed as a criminal offence. If you were found out and by some chance the company decided to keep you on. just consider what would have happened to your credibility and standing with your employer. Most companies would just fire you and they would be well within their rights to call the police.

I firmly believe in telling the truth in job seeking situations. I think you should present yourself in the best possible light and I think this can only be done with the truth. I also believe that if you cannot find in your history the right experiences for the job you are applying for then you should not be applying for it. If you don't have the right experience it is not an issue, all it means is that you need to find a few other jobs that will give you that experience. Remember, you can apply this system as many times as you like, so go get the experience and then apply for the job you want.

I have found in many cases people have all the right experience but just don't realise, or they don't know how to articulate it on their CV, or are not good at making the links for the interviewer. Again, let me give you a brief example.

Jo was a woman who was returning to work after a career break to raise her children. She came to me because she had applied for hundreds of secretarial positions and had not got even an interview. When I looked at her CV it showed a big gap for the ten years she had been raising her children.

When I asked Jo about that gap, she told me about the charity work she had done, the Parent Teacher Association she chaired and the local Neighbourhood Watch she was involved with. On top of this she was looking after her own children, had arranged for a group of local mothers to support each other with things from shopping to babysitting. Within minutes I recognised Jo as an incredible organisational wizard.

We rearranged her CV and got her applying for jobs as a PA. She applied for five more jobs, got interviewed for three of them and was offered the first and the best for her. This is not untypical of the results you can expect when you apply the whole of this system.

There is no reason to lie or cheat to get your ideal job. You just need to present your experience properly and relate it to the role you are going for. The system will take care of the rest.

The next chapter is about the misconceptions that centre on job hunting. The most important thing you need to get your ideal job is the right attitude. Cultivate this and everything else falls into place. The easiest way to develop this is by understanding where the power is when you are in interview. The next chapter will give you the understanding that is vital to becoming the perfect interview candidate.

The Misconceptions of Job Hunting

I n this chapter we will examine some of the mistaken beliefs about applying for a job. We will look at what companies say they want, what they really want and some golden nuggets that will allow you to shift the balance of power in your favour.

This is probably the most important chapter in this book. It sets out the guiding principles, fundamental concepts and key ideas that all the other techniques and skills are built on. Whilst there are no exercises, things to do or direct applications in this chapter, take the time to go through it, understand it and integrate the ideas into the way you approach companies.

Does your face fit and can you do the job?

Having been an employer I have seen many interview candidates who through words, deeds and actions seem as if they are begging for a job. Imagine an extreme example. Let's say you are looking to employ an individual for a key role that is going to make a significant difference to your business. A guy walks into interview, their CV looks reasonable but they beg for the job. Would you be confident in their ability to do the job?

Let's take a contrary example. What if a guy with the same relevant experience on their CV walks in, relaxed, confident and asking you for reasons for why they should agree to take the job? How would you feel about them compared to the first?

My experience as an employer was that I got lots more of the former and not enough of the latter, and it made a significant difference to how I perceived the candidate. As an employer my primary concerns are getting the work done and fitting with the company ethos. In short, "Does your face fit and can you do the job?"

We will come back to that phrase a lot through this book. The intention is to demonstrate a positive answer at every stage of the selection process. But we want to go much further than just that.

What are interviews actually about?

Let me give you two typical categories of job seeking chumps. The first is the one I alluded to above, those who come in cap in hand begging for a job. Their interviews are about pleading and telling you how "they will try their best".

The second category of job seeking chump is the arrogant one. Usually it's false bravado, but the real scary ones are those who actually believe it. This category of job seekers includes the ones that come in and spend all their time telling you how great they are.

Both these two categories have something in common that really hinder them getting a job. They believe the interview is about them. It's not.

Remember that phrase in the section above, "Does your face fit and can you do the job?" The whole CV/résumé writing, the interview and anything else involved in the job selection process is about the company and how you can fulfil their needs.

Neither begging nor bragging will get you a job. Explaining or, even better, demonstrating to your recruiter how you will far exceed their expectations of the role and bring the company a massive return on investment is what is needed. Any system we use needs to demonstrate this to the recruiter at every stage of the recruitment process.

The best person for the job?

I don't think anyone but the most naive of HR Assistants really believes the job selection process gives them the best person for the job. What you get are the people who are best at presenting themselves at interview getting the job. Our task is to make sure that you are not only a good candidate for the position (hopefully the best, but we can't count on that entirely) but certainly the best at presenting themselves through the job selection process.

Balance of power

Companies hire people on skills and experience, but they fire people for attitude. When a recruiter is paper sifting CVs or résumés they generally look for relevant experience, qualifications and skills. This is because these are what is recorded on a CV, they can be measured and talked about.

The reality, though, is attitude is the more important factor. An employer can train people in skills, they can give their staff the right experience and send them to college for the qualifications. What they can't do easily is fiddle with people's attitudes so that they align with the company values. And worse still, most of the people problems in companies are about attitude.

Taking on the wrong people is hugely expensive for companies. Often once they are in, employment legislation makes it difficult to get rid of them (quite correctly in my book, it should not be the employee's fault for being hired inappropriately). Add to this the drop in productivity of that employee, the cost of recruiting them in the first place then having to recruit their replacement. Not to mention tying up the time of all the people that have to be involved in the hiring and firing process.

Employers are terrified of employing the wrong person. They profit considerably from getting the right person. But they often don't know what they are actually looking for.

Now consider this: you apply for a job that you know you would be great for, it is either an ideal role for you or at least a stepping stone in the right direction and you are prepared to contribute to the success of the company and thereby your own. If all this is true, that organisation should be beating a path to your door begging you to take their job.

Your responsibility with using this system is to go only for jobs that you want. It either has to be your ideal job right now or a job that is a stepping stone to where you want to go. Once you have worked this system, built your confidence with it and set yourself free from worrying about getting jobs, you will suddenly realise that these are the only jobs worth applying for. Although, like me, you might get to a point where you go for job interviews purely for the fun and practice.

Right now, throw away the begging bowl, develop a confident swagger and start to understand the piece of rhetoric lots of companies trot out: "Our people are our most valuable asset". Many companies say that sort of thing, I don't know how many of them actually understand the implications... but right now I want you to understand that it is really true and that means in a job hunting scenario you hold the balance of power.

A fair exchange of values

A lot of companies talk about loyalty. They often "give you" opportunities to expand your experience, gain qualifications or, my personal favourite, give you an interesting job in exchange for company loyalty. The reality of being an employee is that there is a fair exchange of values. You contract to give a company your time, effort and expertise in exchange for the things you want, which probably include money but should include many other things like those above as well.

At the point where the exchange is no longer fair, i.e. the company does not get what they want or you don't get what you want, then it is the duty of both parties to walk away and do something better.

As an employer I do not want to keep employees that don't give me a return on investment. As an employee I do not want to work in a company where my needs are not met, whether those needs are financial, social, developmental or any other "al" you can think of. This is not about loyalty, just about a fair exchange of values.

As you get more confident with the system you will realise you have the power to get the jobs you want and don't have to be indebted to a company who are "giving you an opportunity" to work for them.

Start thinking about the job you want and about a fair exchange of values. What sorts of things do you want from the company and what are you prepared to give back to get it? Only go for roles where you will have fun, satisfy your needs and do the things you want to do. If you do this you will be putting a lot of energy into the role so the company benefits as well and we have a fair exchange of values.

Hiring on attitude, skills and abilities

In summary:

- Companies hire on skills and fire on attitude
- Companies lose hugely when they employ the wrong person
- The best person doesn't necessarily get the job. The person that best presents themselves through the job selection process gets the job
- Many job seeking chumps walk in with the wrong attitude and focused on the wrong things
- So long as you only go for jobs where you have a fair exchange of values, you are holding the balance of power

As we go through the job hunting system you will find that there are a number of other misconceptions that we need to challenge. But this is the core. You hold the power and have control of the situation. All we need to do is make it count.

In the next chapter we will talk through how to create a job winning personality.

A Job Winning Personality

The object of the next two chapters is to give you the tools to create the ultimate job winning personality. We will start in this chapter by looking at why this is important and what a job winning personality looks like. In the next chapter we will talk about how you create one. But no peeking ahead because it is important that you understand why and what before we look at how you create one.

Lessons from my youth – attitude is everything (almost)

Let me give you a personal example of how important attitude can be in a job hunting situation.

Many years ago at university I was on a degree course where you had to gather work experience throughout your degree. Being 19 and wanting to spend the summer travelling around Europe, I was less than enthusiastic about applying for engineering jobs. Unfortunately, my university had found me a company that wanted to interview me for a job in their research and development department.

This left me in a situation where I did not want the job but I would get into trouble with my lecturers if I was not seen to put the effort into getting it. I hatched a cunning plan. If I went into the interview all arrogant and self important surely they would not want to employ me. I knew there was only one position and the university had put three students, including me, forward. I only had to be a little worse than the other two.

On the day of the interview I power dressed, pumped up my confidence and swaggered into the interview room. There was only one interviewer, the man I would be directly working for. After the opening pleasantries, but before the interviewer could get started, I opened with a question of my own. It was something like, "As one of the best students on my course, how will I benefit from working in your company?"

Imagine the situation from the interviewer's perspective. He has or will see two other guys who are typical 19-year old students with their begging bowls pleading for a job. Instantly, I am looking very different and I have shifted the balance of power.

Also note, the question contains a presupposition (more about what they are later but for the moment assumptions hidden in the question). I made the statement that I am one of the best students and followed it through with a question which, if answered, presupposes that I am one of the best students in the mind of the interviewer. This works, regardless of any evidence. If, at the age of nineteen, I had had any clue about what I was doing this would have been very clever.

A good interviewer would have taken back control by reframing and asking a question back (don't worry we will show you how to control the interview in a later section as well). Unfortunately, in fifteen years of looking at interview situations I have only seen a handful of good interviewers.

This poor guy was taken completely off balance and he tried to justify the experience I would be getting by showing me all the interesting research projects I would be involved with. My natural curiosity and problem-solving nature came into play and I started offering comments, ideas and solutions to the projects he showed me.

Again, let's look at this from the interviewer's perspective. Suddenly he has had his interview derailed by a confident young man who is prepared to speak his mind, is full of ideas and is completely absorbed in the work that he would be employed for.

At the end of the hour the interviewer apologised, told me that was all the time we had for the interview and showed me out. I thought I had done a brilliant job of not getting the job. Let's face it, I had managed to sidetrack the interviewer; we had not discussed any of my CV, experience or qualifications. Imagine my shock, horror and disgust when he phoned a couple of hours later and gave me the position.

It was only years later when I was studying interviews that the significance of my experience really hit me. By accident – I knew nothing about interview technique at the time – I developed an attitude that almost guaranteed that I got the job.

There is more to it than just having the right attitude, but you will find that if you have this everything else will follow. Some of the things I will ask you to do in interview are really hard if you don't have the right attitude. Conversely when you get the attitude right all the things I am asking you to do will come naturally.

So let's have a quick look at the theory, discover what the right attitude is and then work out how you can get it.

What's inside leaks out

People are like icebergs. You can see what they do, the behaviour they show and the results that they get. But all of this is driven but things you can't see, their values, beliefs and, my catch all term, their attitude. Here is a simple example:

Let's imagine a person going for a job who thinks they are worthless, that there are many better people than them applying for the job and that the interviewer will be biased against them. In my hypothetical example it is likely that this person is going in already defeated. They may not have researched the company as thoroughly as they could have. They might not have thought up questions that challenge the interviewer or worked out how *they* would benefit the company before the interview. What would be the point, they won't get the job anyway?

In the interview they might spend time staring at the floor, not making eye contact and giving the appearance of someone with no confidence. They are unlikely to be engaging, curious or excited about the position. If they have not done enough research they are not going to come across as interested in the company.

This person has managed to lose the job simply because of their attitude. Before you think that someone putting on an over-confident, bragging personality would do any better, let's look at another hypothetical example.

Imagine someone so conceited that they think they are God's gift to the world, everything they do is gold and that they are perfect at everything. Then imagine being the person who interviews them. How much rapport do you think they will build? Are they likely to engage with the interview process, demonstrate their ability to do the role or evidence their skills? It is my contention that they are unlikely to do any of these things. Again, the way they are thinking on the inside is likely to have a direct impact to how they are perceived on the outside, i.e. by other people.

So what is the job winning personality?

How would you act if you were:

- Only applying for the job because you thought you would enjoy it
- The perfect person for the role and you could give the company ten times their return on investment in you
- But the company knew nothing about you?

My guess is that you would be relaxed, confident and wanting to give the company the opportunity to see your greatness and employ you.

How is this as a starter for ten on a good job winning personality?

I want to add an extra twist. If you were going around telling people how great you are, there is the chance you would be labelled arrogant, a braggart and people might not believe you. So let's just add that you are not allowed to tell people directly how good you are, all you are allowed to do is demonstrate your brilliance in words, deed and actions by citing specific examples.

Let's see what that would like to an interviewer. If there are many companies that would want you and you are happy with what you can contribute, no one job is that important and therefore your interview nerves will have disappeared. So walking into the interview you are relaxed, confident and engaging. Throughout the interview you give examples of your ability to make the company profit or save them money. You ask intelligent questions and make the interviewer work hard to justify why you should work for them over any other company.

Is this starting to look like an attitude that will get you the job? I hope so because it has worked for a whole lot of my coaching clients.

The next chapter is all about creating that personality, but before you move on, spend a few moments imagining how you would act if this personality were in place already.

Developing The Attitude

I n this chapter we will look at how you can create the ideal job winning personality that we started looking at in the last chapter. You will return to this chapter several times. Initially, just have a skim through and see what is involved. If you have a role in mind, run through the exercises as they are. When you have a specific job advertisement to apply for, run through these exercises again adding the extra detail. Finally, the day before interview, just run through these exercises again making sure you can demonstrate all the things that make you a perfect candidate for the role.

The story so far

Let me ask you a question. We have not talked about CVs and résumés, we have not got close to talking about interviews, we are barely past the start of the book and I am talking about the attitude that will get you a job. Have you stopped to consider why?

It's because we are looking at an overall process for getting you the right job. For you to walk into the interview with the "right" attitude, you should start the system up the right way. And that means your attitude needs to be "right" right from the start.

The good news is, I have been setting you up over the first few chapters to start developing the "right" attitude. Remember we had a whole chapter on the misconception of job hunting. Think about the number of times I have already asked you to look through the eyes of the interviewer. In the last chapter we compared arrogant and defeated job seekers with a relaxed, confident person. All of this was designed to start shifting you away from the traditional mentality around job seeking to a new, more dynamic and powerful approach.

If you can understand the concepts, consider how they apply to you and imagine how you would be able to behave differently in an interview, we are already most of the way there.

Throughout this chapter we are going to look at exercises that allow you to develop these ideas more fully.

But first some NLP and hypnosis concepts

For the NLP and hypnosis jargon junkies out there, the final exercise below is a variation on a technique called Perceptual Positions. If you want to know more about that, just google it on the internet and you will find hundreds of articles explaining the ins and outs of this exercise. What we will discuss is why it is the most important exercise in this whole book.

The biggest misconception in job seeking is that people believe their CV/résumé writing and interviews are all about themselves. They are not, they are all about demonstrating your value to the company and the company demonstrating their value to you. The exercises below lead you through first examining the values issue and then looking at the ideal interview candidate through the eyes of both the interviewer and your own eyes.

By being able to imagine the interview through these various "perceptual positions" you can gain several insights, the most obvious being key details about how you need to act and what an interviewer needs to hear for you to demonstrate how good you are for the job.

But equally important, how it feels to be delivering a really good interview. This is a huge step to calming those interview nerves – but we will talk about that more in a later chapter.

The more you can imagine this situation, the more your mind gets used to acting this way, to the point where eventually you become very comfortable acting this way in interview. The final exercise will give you a foundation that will serve you well time and time again, and not just in job hunting situations. So, without further ado let's start going through it.

Is this job worth it?

Earlier I suggested that it is important that you only apply for jobs that will genuinely give you the outcomes that you want. These might just be the money and/or location, but this system becomes more powerful when you see the job as rewarding, enjoyable, perhaps with potential for your development (career, skills, personal – one, some or all of these).

It doesn't matter if you think you only want the job for a few months, that you only want a specific piece of experience before you move on, or that you will hate the job but it is important for your long term career goals. All that is important is that you will get things that are important to you from this job.

Whether you are after a type of role or have a specific job advertisement to apply for, spend a few moments working out why this job is important to you. Here is why this is a good exercise.

Imagine yourself as an interviewer, you have two candidates in front of you and you ask them why they applied for the job. You get these two answers respectively:

"Any job will do, I just need the money to survive."

"Out of all the companies and jobs that I could choose I picked yours because I like (fill in what you like about the company), my long term career path is to be (x) and this is a role where I can develop (y) experience."

Which of these candidates would you be more impressed with?

Knowing and being able to articulate what you want from the role makes you a much stronger candidate.

List the things you want to get from the job.

Are you worth it to the company?

What will make you shine in an interview is demonstrating how much value you can bring to the company. Before applying for any role it makes sense to be able to evidence the qualities that you will bring to it that would make you the perfect candidate. Ideally I am looking for ten times your salary as a return of investment to the company. Imagine the interview where before it starts you calmly evidence how the company will make ten times your asking salary back when they hire you. I suspect the interview would end right there and you would be working for them the very next day.

If you are back from your daydream, I do recognise that the situation may not be as clear cut and simple as that... but your job right now is to work your way through what it is that the company will get from employing you. If you don't think it's enough then you should not be going for the job.

Before we leave the subject I want to make sure you are assessing your skills effectively, so let me give some real examples of assessing qualities for a role.

Remember Jo in chapter one. She had secretarial skills that were ten years old, but her recent experience was all about multitasking, organising a hectic lifestyle and several people efficiently as well as persuading and leading various groups where she didn't have any organisational power. Jo didn't recognise it at first, but this is just perfect evidence of a brilliant PA.

Dave was going for a job where he had little or no experience and he was 19 whilst the average age for the role was late 20s. Dave's main contribution to the company was a fresh pair of eyes untainted by years of doing things the way they had always done them, as well as youthful energy and ambition. Particularly when you looked on the company website and they clearly stated they were after energetic, ambitious and creative people. Dave simply exhibited all the qualities the company were looking for.

Kevin was seeking his first job after completing his degree. He was aiming for a graduate fast track management role. He had good grades from his engineering degree but was still struggling to get interviews. The reality is that lots of people leave university with good grades, but this alone is not enough because many student and graduate CVs look very similar.

Kevin looked at all the extracurricular activities he had been involved with. He then looked at the management roles he would typically be in after five years of a graduate fast track scheme. He then wrote up his CV connecting his experience to the skills he would need in that management role. All of a sudden his CV looked dramatically different from most and gave much more than just a list of qualifications with a study break to go travelling. He got offered five interviews from the next six applications and from those five interviews was offered three placements.

List what the company will get from you.

What does the perfect candidate look like?

You now have two lists. The first is what you will get from the role and the second list is what the company will get from you. The third exercise is a little more complex and needs you to use your imagination a little.

I want you to imagine someone (not yourself) doing the job that you want. The more you know about the job the better but this exercise works even if you only know the job superficially. If you don't know the job at all then find out before applying.

In your imaginary world, notice the skills, abilities and qualities this person has to be able to do the job really well. If you are applying to a specific company, find out about their culture, values and ways of working (the internet will give you this in moments for a large number of companies). How does your ideal person exhibit the company values? The more effectively you can imagine this, the better quality results you will get.

Now that you can imagine the perfect person doing the job let's change the scene. Imagine that same person sitting in the interview that got them the job. Imagine yourself as the interviewer: what would they have to say to you to convince you that they will be brilliant at the job? What behaviour and actions in the interview will inspire confidence that they will be good in the job? Spend the time really thinking this through in as much detail as you can.

Once you have started getting a sense of how the perfect candidate can demonstrate their ability in interview, slowly change their features to look like you. Now you are imagining seeing yourself in the interview demonstrating how perfect you are for the role.

Once you have this well imagined from the interviewer's perspective, watch it again from an external perspective – i.e. you can see both the interviewer and yourself. From this position imagine the rapport between the interviewer and the interviewee; notice how they are in tune with each other; and just notice the interviewee – that you, even if you are looking from the outside – is calm, collected and in control.

For the final part of this exercise, step into your own body and look at the situation through your own eyes. Imagine what it is like to feel this way in interview, giving the answers that demonstrate how good you are for the job and being confident that you are the perfect candidate (remember that is where we started this exercise).

When you are ready, come back to the real world and notice that you now have what the ideal candidate would say and do in interview for the interviewer to recognise how good they are. Just as importantly, you also know what it feels like to be doing that interview as the perfect candidate. Obviously the more detail you can add, the better the results you will get. This is why you should do this exercise regularly as you get more information.

Ideally, if you know the interviewer, have spent time with the people who do the job and can see the interview room ahead of schedule then this exercise can be very powerful. But even if you have to make up all the details yourself there is significant benefit in this exercise.

Mind before body

In this chapter we have ended up with an exercise to start developing the mindset of the ideal candidate for the job and started looking at how that person would act in an interview. We have then started to look at visualisation techniques to mentally rehearse your interviews. This is important because you will need to start practising being this person so you can do it in interview.

Let me clear up one common comment that I sometimes get at this stage. "Am I practising being someone I am not?" I would suggest that if you can't see yourself being the ideal person in the role then you should not be applying for the job. All we are really doing is using your imagination to bring out the qualities within you that are the best for the role. And then we are using your mind to mentally rehearse those "best bits". It might not feel natural initially because those might not be the elements of yourself that you are most familiar with. But if it feels fake, then you are probably heading for the wrong job.

Remember, we discussed the idea that it is not the best person for the job that gets the job. It is the person who presents themselves best at interview. That means there is a little more to build into the interview persona, but we will do that a little closer to the interview stage. For the moment, start rehearsing the interview as the ideal candidate because we have work to do on your CV or résumé.

In the next chapter we are going to look at what CVs and résumés are, common misconceptions about them and then we will look at the anatomy of a hypnotically persuasive CV or résumé.

Anatomy of a Hypnotic CV or Résumé

I n this chapter we will look at what a CV or résumé is, what it does and some common misconceptions about them. We will then have a look at a typical example and a hypnotically persuasive CV.

Some people might believe that they can skip this chapter and get into the next couple of chapters about creating your own CV or résumé. I urge you to stay with this chapter. Because by understanding all the core elements, letting go of the common misconceptions and learning how we are building up your CV/résumé into part of a Job Winning System you can tweak the process to work even better for you personal circumstances.

What is a CV or a résumé?

If you have a look around the internet you will find hundreds of tiresome definitions of CVs and résumés. You will find many different types and many people with their self imposed rules about what sort to use for which sort of situation. You will find different types of content, layout and even purposes for these things. For this reason we are going back to basics and building up our own version of what a CV or résumé is, from what we want it to do.

So what is the purpose of a CV or résumé?

Our CV or résumé is only going to be for two purposes. The first is to get an interview and the second is to layout the initial conditions so we can take covert control of that interview.

Initially the CV or résumé is just a sales document. It is there to present you as the best solution to the problem of having the vacancy. Like any complex product, you would not expect to buy from just a sales brochure. The document needs to say you are such a good potential solution that the company have to call in the sales agent (that would be you) to discuss whether the product (that is you again) is the best solution.

I want your CV or résumé to do a little more than just get people to want to call you for interview. I want the document to do the ground work to allow you to take covert control of the interview. There is more to covert control than just this element, but the ground work that a CV can do for you is to completely cover the topics you will discuss in interview and the content of all of your answers.

In summary, our CV or résumé is a sales document to get you the interview and lays out the content for you to use to take covert control of the interview. On a final note, the difference between a CV and a résumé: well the internet will lay out lots of complex differences, but for us, Americans use the term résumé and Brits use the term CV. For our purposes both are just a sales document to get you the interview and allow you to take covert control of that interview. For brevity, and because it is what I am most used to, I am just going to use the term CV from here on.

A hypnotic CV in action

Let's look at worst case scenarios for a moment. Imagine being a recruiter, you have one position to fill and a thousand applicants all of whom have fairly similar CVs. The chances are you will do an initial paper sift that quickly scans the first page looking for things that either count that person in or count that person out. This means, for a CV to stand a chance it needs to look a little different, draw the eye to a place on the document where there is a statement that makes the candidate look perfect for the job. This will ensure that the candidate goes on the count **in** pile.

So now you have paper sifted to a more manageable pile you are likely to look at the CVs more closely. Let's say you have your one thousand CVs down to one hundred and you have decided that you will interview five. The chances are you will do the two piles thing again, but just looking a little more closely at each CV. You might, but it is unlikely that you will, travel further than the front page of any of the CVs.

This time, for the CV to stand a chance it needs to bear up to closer scrutiny. For this section, let's say the front page contains a big, bold statement that matches the job criteria and company profile exactly. This would mean the CV would be kept in the **include** pile.

Perhaps as the recruiter, you might now have whittled it down to ten CVs and you will still interview only five. Now you might look at the CVs more closely and even start putting them in order of preference. Imagine a CV where all of the most important elements are on the front page (so none of it is missed), it has bold statements that match the company and the job, but as well as all of this the fine detail supports and provides evidence of those statements. I think a CV like that is likely to appear high in your top five. If your CV can stand up to this test then most paper sift process will be even easier. So, without further ado, let's take a closer look at the elements of a CV.

The elements of a hypnotic CV in detail

In the front of this book you will find a web address where you can log in and get your free bonuses, one of which is this CV/Résumé template.

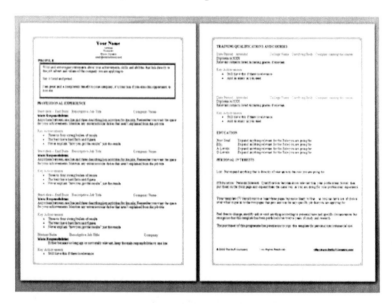

I have deliberately kept this picture small so you can't read the writing. Stay calm, we will get to what the writing should say in a little while, but first I want you to understand how this CV works.

Here are some of the key points.

It is only two pages long, and anything that is important for the job should appear on the first page. When you get to write your CV for the first time I would expect that you come up with about four pages of material. This will give you lots to select from when you chop it down to the two pages that you will send to companies.

When you download the template you will notice that the border is in a light grey and there are two different blue colours used for the box out, headings and sub headings. All of this is calculated to make your CV stand out slightly from the usual without it being too strange. Research shows that blue is the most trusted and accepted colour so it makes sense to use blue when we stray away from traditional black on white writing.

CONTACT DETAILS

At the top of the page is your name and contact details. This is the traditional place to put this stuff. The reality is that the recruiter has no need of this information until they decide to contact you. So for the more non traditional companies you might even consider putting just your name on the front and the rest of your contact details on the back page. For the sake of conformity I have left this on at the top of the front page for your template.

One thing to be aware of is "isms". Certainly in the UK, bias against race, gender, sexual orientation, disability and age are all alive and well. Names and contact details can easily give away details that may get you paper sifted out.

A Sikh friend of mine uses his "British" nickname on CVs and he gets a better response than when he uses his real name. You may consider using this approach or not putting on any details that give away your gender, ethnicity, age or disability. Another approach, which won't get you the job but would make me happy, is to split test by sending in CVs that slightly differ in these areas. If one gets offered an interview and the other doesn't I would just report them to the appropriate authorities.

I would also turn up for the interview and if they query why you are not named the same as your CV I would tell them and also explain to them the reasons. But let's face it, if they are discriminating in this way they are likely to find ways to not hire "one of them" particularly if they are a "trouble maker". So you probably won't get the job. I would turn up to make them sweat about being found out but perhaps we all have better things to do with our time.

The great thing about this system, though, is you don't need to pander to the whims of employers. Remember you are looking for the jobs where you will be brilliant and to a large degree you are going to be calling the shots.

PROFILE BOX

Notice how straight after the contact details is a blue box. This is your Profile box and is the most customisable and important part of your CV. This is the bit you want your recruiter to read if they read anything. This is why it is where it is and why it has a blue border surrounding it.

We will talk about this box in more detail in the next section, but for the moment just assume it will contain hypnotic trance words to draw the reader in, wild and extravagant statements about how great you will be in the role and huge benefit statements that let the recruiter know that they will be blessed for recruiting you. We will of course be telling the truth about you, so if anything in this paragraph makes you quake, reread the previous chapter on attitude.

PROFESSIONAL EXPERIENCE

The next section is your professional experience. Notice how this is laid out. Here is a close up of this section so you can see.

I am great and a completely benefit to your company, it's your loss if you miss this opportunity to hire me.

PROFESSIONAL EXPERIENCE

Start date – End Date   Descriptive Job Title   Company Name
Main Responsibilities:
Anywhere between one line and three describing key activities for the role. Remember you want the space for your achievements. Mention any extra curricular duties that aren't explained from the job title

Key Achievements
- Three to four strong bullets of results
- The best have hard facts and figures
- Never explain "how you got the results" just the results

Start date – End Date   Descriptive Job Title   Company Name
Main Responsibilities:
Anywhere between one line and three describing key activities for the role. Remember you want the space for your achievements. Mention any extra curricular duties that aren't explained from the job title

Key Achievements
- Three to four strong bullets of results
- The best have hard facts and figures

Notice the title of this section is Professional Experience. You can use any words you want to head up this section but make sure that it reflects your status, professionalism and attitude. The only people that have "work experience" are 15 year-olds on release from their school. Other titles that work well include: Career Highlights/Achievements (if you are not listing everything); Key Achievements (if listing experience outside a work related scenario). I prefer Professional Experience as I think it sets the right tone for how the recruiters should be thinking about you.

Notice after this the company name, job title and dates – then main responsibilities are kept as short as possible. This is because this is of no real consequence. The really important messages are the bullet points called "Key Achievements".

Think about this from an employer's perspective. Do you want someone who just does a job or do you want someone who really pulls the business forward by going the extra mile, using their initiative to drive the business forward and any other corporate-speak phrases that mean you are better for the role than those mere candidates that have their begging bowls out?

Don't worry, in the next couple of chapters I will show you how you can turn the most mundane experience into blistering, key pieces of experience that say you were born for the job you are applying for. If you have not already guessed, this section is where you also support the wild and extravagant statements you made earlier.

EVERYTHING ELSE

The final part of the CV is page two and the correct term for it is "everything else". This might include qualifications, training, personal interests and all the usual things a CV might have. Incidentally, this is one area where I think résumés are different. On a résumé it is often appropriate to reduce it to one page and leave all this stuff out. On a CV it would look a little odd if this page was not included.

But in either case, if there is anything important and relevant to the job you are applying for it should appear on the front page. Remember the worst case scenario, you will have to pass through two paper sifts before anyone actually reads much of your CV. If it is important it must be on the front page.

For example, you have had a working career in engineering and reached the giddy heights of Operations Director. But now you want a career change and you are applying for jobs as an underwater basket weaver. You have worked out that the key skills that underwater basket weavers need are being able to hold their breath and have nimble fingers. You scuba dive and embroider as hobbies, both clearly showing the key skills required for your new role. All of a sudden your CV front page will be all about your personal interests and your professional history, however glorious, will be relegated to the back page.

How your hypnotic CV or résumé will work

Over the next couple of chapters we will look at constructing the content of your CV, but what you can see from this chapter is the general outline of how this system works. Your CV with the borders and boxes will look slightly different from most. Not so different as to make you look like a complete renegade but different enough to make you stand out.

Incidentally, if you are snail mailing your CV to places then print it on slightly thicker, good quality paper so it feels different as well. You may also want to consider putting it in a card wallet. This might get to be impractical if you are sending out lots of CVs but if you are only sending a few then making the whole thing special is an effort worth making.

Now that your CV looks and feels a little different you dramatically increase the chances of it being looked at. The first thing that an employer or recruiter will look at is the big blue box on the front. In a couple of chapters' time I will show you how you can fill that box with hot buttons that almost guarantee that they will want to read further. Everything in this box will make you look like you were born for the position and that the company will really be missing out by not at least interviewing you.

You may get the interview just on that basis, but a hard bitten, cynical or even just conscientious recruiter may read the rest of the CV. When they do they will find the rest of the front page supports all the wild and extravagant statements in the profile box. They may look at the second page, but who cares? Everything that is important is on the front.

Remember this is a system; that front page is setting the recruiter up for what will happen to them in the interview.

We are getting a little ahead of ourselves, but this is important. What we put on the front page of that CV will set up the content you will deliver in the interview. You will dramatically increase your believability factor (not that I am asking you to lie, it's just that most interviewees do not come over as believable even when they are telling the truth). You will also be able to prepare your answers, know what will come up in interview and take complete control of the interview situation.

As you may well have guessed, this CV or résumé is the very foundation of the whole Job Hunting System so in the next chapter we will start to discuss how to create a compelling CV that makes you look as if you are born for the role.

Writing Your Winning CV or Résumé Part One: Professional Experience

I n this chapter we will look in how to create your CV. We will look at your experience through the eyes of a potential employer and how we can frame it to show you in the best possible light. In this chapter you will generate lots of content for your CV, in the next chapter you will hone and customise that content to fit specific companies or roles

Before we start I want you to recognise two things. Firstly, a CV is just a sales document and its only purpose is to get you to, and set you up for, the interview. The second thing I want you to keep focused on is a really common mistake many job seeking chumps make. We've discussed it before but let's make this absolutely clear. This CV is not about you, it is only about the company/role. Or, to be specific, it is about how you (the product) can provide benefit to the company. If you don't keep these two ideas in mind you will not be able to write a winning CV.

In the next few pages we will go through a system to generate the content for your CV and relate it directly to the role and the companies you want to apply for. Take your time going through this; it is the bedrock of your job hunting system. Getting this right will make the rest flow easily. The most successful job hunters I have coached have spent at least a week working on their CVs and still constantly tinker with them. Consider it this way, if this CV leads to your ideal job and from there you can use it to consistently upgrade your job, is it worth taking a little time to get it right?

Perceptual positions revisited

We are now going to look through your life, experiences and qualifications in relation to the ideal candidate for the job to generate some content for your winning CV.

Way back in the chapter on developing the attitude, we did a perceptual positions exercise about the ideal person for the role. I would like you to revisit that exercise and as you do it again just note down the key skills and experience the ideal person would have.

Once you have some general ideas, get yourself into a nice relaxed state as we are going to do a little more visualisation. Imagine yourself in a big comfy chair, remote control in hand and a big screen in front of you. In your mind just play back your last few years searching for the experiences that demonstrate the key skills that you need for you new role.

All you are looking for are experiences that relate to the type of job you are going for, they could come from anywhere. Here are a few examples I have seen working with people.

A guy wanting his first sales role remembered a time when he convinced his college lecturer to allow him to submit an assessed essay that was slightly outside the normal brief. He sold the idea in to his lecturer.

A young woman wanting to become a police officer realised that as a call centre team leader she had considerable leadership skills. She then managed to hone down on a couple of experiences that really demonstrated her taking control of a situation that could have got out of hand. One dealt with an advisor that she had to sack who was getting increasingly angry in the interview. She talked him down, got him calm and escorted him out of the building. Doesn't that sound like the key skills a police officer should have?

Another example was a general business manager with a strong financial customer service background looking to apply for a role requiring strong time and project management skills. Whilst she could demonstrate a lot of these skills in work, a great achievement for her was a particular time when she was directing a play for her amateur dramatic company, dealing with two separate work projects and caring for her young family. She tells me she got the job on the basis of retelling this one event.

This should give you some idea of the sort of thing you are looking for. Now all you want to do is just make a note of key experiences in your life that directly relate to the skills that are appropriate for the role you want to go for. These experiences are going to form the bulk of your interview answers and are going to be seeded through your CV.

In the next section you will learn how to put together your professional experiences in a way that draws the reader in, makes you look like you were born for the job and sets you up to deliver killer interview answers regardless of what questions you are asked. But before we do that there is a key concept you need to get a good grip on.

Tasks versus achievements

A task is a routine activity that you undertake. An achievement is a one-off event with a defined and preferably amazing result. Step back into your potential employer's shoes. Do you want someone who has a list of daily routine activities or do you want someone who has achieved things in their previous roles. On many CVs I have seen the focus is far too strongly on lists of routine activities.

Often at this point I am given an objection like, "But all I do in my job is routine activities". My usual answer to this is to say for most people this is not the case and they just don't know where to look. If you really don't have any achievements then I would suggest you stay in the same job for another six months achieving something before moving on.

Let's assume you have probably achieved quite a lot and don't yet recognise it. Here are a few things to think about. Have you ever been commended or complimented by your boss, your peers or by a customer – in fact by anybody? If you have then there is an achievement behind it.

Do you have a job where you have to perform to targets and have achieved them early, over achieved or created an unexpected positive result? Again, there is an achievement there.

Have you failed badly and learnt a really valuable lesson from it that you now always apply? Again a great achievement and often painfully won. Why not let it work for you on your CV?

The idea here is looking at events and moving the boundaries until you see the great result you have got from them. Let me give you a few examples, some of which are extreme, just to prove the point that most events can give you a positive achievement.

I have coached a few ex-convicts in job hunting skills. One thing that is bound to come up is the big hole in their CV. By law they have to declare they were in prison and usually they have studied, worked on their personal development or spent their time getting/

keeping fit. All of these could be couched in terms of achievements. Whilst being an ex-convict is never going to be a positive boost to your CV, you can still highlight key achievements that have come from it.

As a side note, pulling off the biggest bank robbery in history is an achievement, but it probably is not one that you should put on your CV. Unless of course it directly relates to the role you are going for, security consultant perhaps?

I have recently been talking with a guy who was made redundant and spent nine months on the dole without getting any interviews. When I discussed how he had been spending his time he told me that he had done some charity work, read a few books and had taken up gardening.

When I explored this further I found out that the charity work involved organising and helping out in a shop, as a result the shop was making more sales. This is an achievement.

The books that he had been reading were about sales and sales management (the role he was going for). So despite being redundant he was updating his skills and professional development. But the key thing is he took some ideas from the books he was reading and applied them to the charity shop. Again a big achievement, despite being out of work he took his professional development and applied it to create a result.

The gardening you could just reframe as taking up a new hobby, but when I explored it with him I found out that he was tending three gardens, his own and two of his neighbours'. Now I have a key achievement demonstrating great time and project management skills. This guy was tending three gardens over a nine month period whilst also job searching, creating results for a charity shop and developing his professional skills.

Here is my point: before I spoke to this guy his CV finished with the job he was made redundant from. He had two interviews before he had spoken to me. In both, when asked about the nine months he told them he had been keeping busy reading, gardening and helping out in a charity shop.

After speaking to me he got offered the job in the very next interview. The key thing that had changed was in interview he blew them away with the amount he had achieved in the nine months he had been redundant and he could relate it all to the sales manager role he was applying for.

I want you to think about the jobs that you have had and start listing your achievements. As best you can, be specific. Numbers always make things seem more real. If you don't have hard numbers use approximates and just say "approximately". If you were part of a team that created the result just list it that way, e.g. "I was part of the team that did (x) resulting in approximately (y) increased sales." Or whatever the result was.

Now you have an understanding of how achievements work better than tasks and you have started looking at some of your experience in relation to the role you are applying for, let us put this all together in terms of your professional experience.

Professional experience

For most people their CV or résumé will cover the work they have done starting with their current job and going back chronologically. But remember, anything that is relevant to the role needs to appear on the front page of your CV.

If, for example, you are making a drastic career change and your hobbies and interests are more relevant than your current job, then you will put your hobbies and interests on the front page, relegating your career history to the second page.

If you were going for a job in a university where your academic experience is vital, this is what would be on the front page. In every one of these cases you will highlight your key achievements in the way we are suggesting below. This is critical to creating your job winning CV and will make it stand out from the crowd.

Here is a quick snap shot of how it should be laid out.

PROFESSIONAL EXPERIENCE

Start date – End Date   Descriptive Job Title   Company Name
Main Responsibilities:
Anywhere between one line and three describing key activities for the role. Remember you want the space for your achievements. Mention any extracurricular duties that aren't explained from the job title

Key Achievements
- Three to four strong bullets of results
- The best have hard facts and figures
- Never explain "how you got the results" just the results

Start date – End Date   Descriptive Job Title   Company Name
Main Responsibilities:
Anywhere between one line and three describing key activities for the role. Remember you want the space for your achievements. Mention any extracurricular duties that aren't explained from the job title

Key Achievements
- Three to four strong bullets of results
- The best have hard facts and figures
- Never explain "how you got the results" just the results

Note that the section is headed Professional Experience. You may prefer Career Achievements or Highlights but just make sure that, whatever you label this section, it sets the right frame and mood for how you want to be treated. So if you want to be consider as 16 years old with no real experience, feel free to call this section your work experience. Of if you want to be thought of as nothing special and lacking any real ability, consider labelling this section career history.

Each employment section is headed with dates, a descriptive job title and the company name. Space is at a premium on the front page so get this on one line. If your actual job title does not reflect what you do then replace it with something that is descriptive. You may have been called Primary Nourishment Engineer but if your role was Tea Boy then use Tea Boy as your descriptive job title.

A common issue that comes up here is people taking on temporary assignments, acting up to a higher grade or taking on projects that are different from their actual job title. In all of these cases just add the word temporary, seconded or whatever appropriately define the nature of your position and keep the descriptive job title.

Think about this from the recruiter's perspective. They don't care what you were called, they just need to know what you were doing and how this relates to the role they are employing you for. Using a descriptive job title makes life easy for everyone.

Underneath the title comes a section labelled Main Responsibilities. A mistake I see often with CVs is the main responsibilities taking huge chunks of space. You should aim to get this into two lines or less and certainly no more than three. The reason being that you want the space to highlight your key achievements.

Again, look at this from a potential employer's perspective. If you have a descriptive job title and two lines clarifying the role, that should be enough to give anyone a flavour of what you did in that job. No one is going to be impressed with lists of duties and tasks and the reality is they don't care what you have done before. What they care about is how you will perform in the new job should you choose to take it. As such you want them to focus on your key achievements.

So underneath the Main Responsibilities is the section

labelled Key Achievements. This should be in bullet point format and range from three to five achievements. There is a point I want you to follow with your key achievements. You should write them in a way that gives the result but not how you achieved it. In NLP and hypnosis terms this is called an open loop.

Open loops the key to drawing people in

Here is a near perfect example of a Key Achievement:

Saved £750,000 pa and increased customer satisfaction by 50% on an engineering redesign that took less than ten minutes.

Don't you just want to know how this guy did this? Imagine you were recruiting design engineers for cost saving projects, would this be a guy you'd want to talk to? If you had this on your CV or résumé you can virtually guarantee this experience will come up and if it doesn't you should bring it up.

The thing about open loops is when you explain the bit that is missing you get a sense of closure or completion. On an unconscious level it feels like a sense of relief; as soon as this key achievement is discussed in the interview you will come across as more credible, believable and your rapport levels will go through the roof.

You should aim to have between at least three and five big key achievements on the front page of your CV that are all linked to the big experiences that demonstrate the key skills for the role.

Hopefully you have already noticed how we are shaping the interview. You might also recognise that you can now start to predict what will come up in the interview and if it doesn't you will bring it up anyway. This method when correctly employed takes the interviewer through a succession of loops. You open them on your CV and close them in the interview.

Let us just go back to looking at this through the eyes of a recruiter. Imagine sifting through a dozen CVs for engineers all detailing how long they have worked, in what companies, what skills they have used and various roles and duties. All of a sudden you see a CV that has five key achievements like the one above and all relevant to the role that they are applying for. Who do you think is going to be interviewed and what do you think will get discussed in that interview?

Key achievements examples

I really want you to get this idea because is it the bedrock of the whole job hunting system. Key achievements that are applicable to the job you are going for, stating specific results and linked to the key experiences you are going to discuss in interview will boost your chances of getting the job immeasurably. So with that in mind, let's look at some more examples of key achievements.

Earlier we discussed a sales manager who had been made redundant and unemployed for nine months. Here is what was on his CV.

July 2008 to Present Professional Development

Main Duties

Following my redundancy I am spending time developing my professional skills whilst searching for my ideal position.

Key Achievements

- Reorganised a charity shop leading to approximately 20% increase in sales
- Developed new sales techniques and tested them in the reorganisation of a charity shop, results as above
- Increased my time and project management skills by taking on three gardening projects, doing charity work and still maintaining a focus on selecting my career path

---

Does this look a little better than having a hole in your Professional Experience or just saying you were redundant? Note some of the interesting language; he is not "looking for a job", he is "selecting a career path".

This little section also has some interesting assumptions hidden it that would be great to bring out during the interview. This person is developing and using his skills. The implications are that he is self managed, takes responsibility for his own development and is good at managing a disparate work load. These are all things that you are expecting a recruiter to notice, but the key is when you get to the interview you can bring them all out as examples and demonstrations of how good a manager you are.

There is a huge open loop here. Anyone who is interested in hiring a sales manager is going to want to know about redesigns and techniques that could increase their sales by 20%.

Also note how he has built this section so that it will become a talking point in interview. This means he can prepare answers and make sure his explanations contain all the key skills looked for in the job he is applying for. Is it any wonder that in the very next interview he is offered the job?

Here are a few more examples of key achievements:

This next example is from a call centre agent who started off saying that she all she did was take calls and didn't have any achievements worth talking about. Again, notice the big open loop as the last key achievement.

04/00 – 08/00 Customer Care Agent

Call Centre

Main Responsibilities

As an agent, my duties were to handle all aspects of customer care during inbound and outbound calls, keeping the standards set by the client and The Call Centre

Key Achievements

- Promoted to QA Specialist after only three months in the organisation

- In three months received two letters of thanks and had three customers request to speak to my manager to pass on compliments about the level of service they received from me

- Saved £3,000 of business through one telephone interaction

In this example the person doesn't explain anything about the role, just how she got it and why she only had it for three months. This is ideal because it is easy to work out what the main functions of a recruitment manager would be. She has two excellent key achievements that open a loop and give some great results. Again this really is setting up the interview discussions.

Feb to April 2005 Interim Recruitment Manager
Multi Site Call Centre
Main Duties

During a period of heavy recruitment we lost the head of department and I stepped in to run the function whilst we found a replacement

Key Achievements

- In three months my team of four recruited 400 people, 42 people promoted and cost of acquisition was reduced by almost 50%

- Implemented new recruitment process and induction process resulting in a 30% drop in probation attrition

---

In this example a teenager was applying to join the Police. He knew one of the things that would be an objection would be his age and subsequent lack of life experience. His original CV just said, "travelled for ten months" as almost a foot note. See what you think of the update he used and notice the open loop appearing again.

September 2002 to June 2003 Personal Development through Travel

I spent 10 months travelling Europe and Asia, exploring living and working in different cultures

Key Achievements

- Successfully aided a severely distressed robbery victim despite not being able to speak the language

- Found work despite being in a completely foreign culture and not speaking the language

- In ten months lived and worked in five countries with very different cultures and norms

---

Now it is your turn

We have spent a fair bit of time discussing your experiences and how you can structure and lay them out in terms of key achievements. So now is the time to start laying out your experiences into a CV format.

I would like to make the exercise a little more difficult for you by adding another dimension of thinking. Remember in the previous chapter we discussed some of the misconceptions of job hunting. One of the key distinctions is the fact that your CV and your interview are not about you. They are all about the relationship between you and the job that you're applying for.

With that in mind, here is a list of generic skills and qualities that companies want in their employees. This list is a fair start and you might want to add any specific skills, attributes or qualities for the role that you are applying for. You should have such a list based on the perceptual positions exercise that you have done earlier.

- Focus / Commitment / Results Driven
- Flexibility / Planning
- Communication Skills
- Creativity
- Initiative / Independence
- Team Player
- Leadership / Management Skills

Take this list and any other key attributes that you consider important and match your experiences and key achievements against them. As you go through this exercise you can start filling in the professional experience section of your CV.

Remember you can apply this approach to any area of your CV. So, for example, if your academic achievements are a vital part of your new role just apply the same approach and layout as above.

By completing this exercise you will have got the idea of how you can structure and present your experience to focus on the key skills that are appropriate to the job that you are going for. But there is one big problem that I will share the solution to in the next chapter. But before you move on, have a go at taking some of your key experiences and set them out in this fashion.

Writing Your Winning CV or Résumé Part Two: Profiles

Now that you've learned to structure and present your experiences as key achievements, we need to deal with one specific problem. Remember our worst-case scenario where we had a recruiter with hundreds of CVs to sift through. We need to have a system where your recruiter will actually read your CV in detail. This chapter is about how you can open that loop.

Already your CV will look different from the norm. This is because of the borders and the way it is laid out. What we are expecting is that people will read your profile. This is because it's at the top of page and is contained within a box of its own. It makes sense then to have this profile exactly match all the requirements of the job that you're applying for.

Our ideal situation is to have the recruiter read the profile box and see a huge amount of connection with the job you are applying for. They then read the front page of your CV in detail and see your open loops, key skills and fantastic achievements.

In this chapter we will focus on creating a profile that draws the recruiter in and makes them want to read the rest of your CV.

Trance words

Before getting into the meat of this chapter I want to give you a little bit of theory that will help you to understand how powerful you can make your profile. Remember, companies tend to hire on skills and experience and they fire people on attitude. The job your profile will do is evidence that you have both the skills and the attitude.

Certain words and phrases connect with us in a deep and unconscious way. There are various categories of words but rather than getting bogged down in theory, we will collect them all together under the term Trance Words. Trance Words are words and phrases that have a deep psychological impact on someone.

Later in the interview section we will discuss how you might use these powerfully with an individual in a face to face or telephone conversation. So we will be coming back to this concept, but for the moment we will discuss how to find and use company Trance Words in your CV and more specifically in your profile.

Have a look at a few company websites. Many of them will have a list of corporate values or a mission statement. Here are a couple of examples that I have just taken straight from some company websites:

Bank

To deliver superior sustainable value we run our business with integrity and openness, delivering optimum financial results within clearly defined business principles.

Computer Manufacturer

In the end, we determined that our actions will be driven by these values:

- Dedication to every client's success
- Innovation that matters, for our company and for the world
- Trust and personal responsibility in all relationships

Three different food retailers

1. Creating value for customers, to earn their lifetime loyalty.
2. Our mission is to be the consumer's first choice for food...at a competitive cost.
3. To be the UK's best value retailer exceeding customer needs. Always.

Using these values in your profile will have an immediate impact on recruiters in those companies. It will feel like you have all the right values to be working for the company. Many large companies have this information splashed all over their websites and it is easy to find.

But what happens if you are going through a recruitment company and you don't know who the employer will be. If nothing else, the recruitment company will give you the industry. All you do is look up several companies from the same industry. Have a look above at the three different food retailers and notice the similarity in the words and phrases that they use; applying similar words and phrases in your profile will appeal to any one of these companies.

But what if I am looking at a company that doesn't openly display their values on the internet? You have two obvious options. Phone and ask them. Have a look at several similar companies and the industry generally, looking for common buzz words and phrases.

By the way, consider how unique you will look to a potential employer if you phone them up and ask them about their company. When they ask why you are asking, tell them you are applying for a job and you would like to know if they are the sort of company you want to work for. This will already set you apart from most job seeking chumps.

By using these words you will appear to have the right attitude to work for the company, but we want to take this a little further. Take hold of a job advertisement/description/specification and you will notice it gives you a list of skills, experience and attributes the company are looking for in their ideal candidate. Here are some extracts from typical job advertisement I have taken from a recruitment site:

Director of Quality and Regulatory Affairs

You are educated to degree calibre in a technical or scientific discipline, and will have proven experience leading and managing a quality and regulatory function in a life sciences manufacturing business. You have expert knowledge and practical experience of CE and FDA regulations, and practical experience of implementing Quality and Regulatory compliance systems within an FDA licensed manufacturing facility. We would be especially keen to hear from candidates with knowledge of the IVD market in general, and specific knowledge of the Immuno-haematology products.

Business Development Manager

To be successful in this role, you will be from a strong Business Development and IT sales background, have excellent self motivation, business knowledge and have a proven track record for delivery of sales with major blue chip IT companies.

Ideally you must be able to display the following skills:

- Daily, Weekly, Monthly forecasting skills
- Proven track record in effective management, campaigns and sales.
- Proven experience in problem solving
- Ability to deal with Senior Management to CEO.
- Adaptability to ever changing marketplace and define clear tactical sales plans.
- Experienced managing and developments of accounts.

Registered Mental Health Nurse

Our client is a high end independent hospital. Their unique approach and outstanding levels of quality care have earned them not only accolades but a very strong reputation and excellent CQC reports.

Due to their continued growth they have an immediate requirement for registered nurses qualified in mental health to join their passionate and fast paced team at one of their fantastic residences in the Merseyside area.

You will be an experienced nurse and most importantly you will be a true advocate of quality care.

You will be NMC registered with a current PIN and willing to undergo a police check against the POVA list.

Notice that these all have a rich source of words and phrases that you can use on your profile. By doing this you are creating a profile that makes you look like you were born for the company and the role. Let's look at how to do this in more detail.

Wild, extravagant and unsupported statements

The only purpose of your profile is to draw the reader in and get them to read the rest of your CV. The easy way to do this is to make sure that your profile matches the job criteria exactly, uses all the company hot buttons or values and makes you look as if you were born for the job.

Your profile can contain as many wild, extravagant and unsupported statements as you like. Consider the impact on anyone reading your CV when you use this approach. If your profile matches the job and contains all the right company buzzwords it will stop them dead in their tracks and make them want to read the rest of your CV. Imagine what then happens to the reader as they go through your professional experience registering all those key achievements that relate directly to the job that they are recruiting for. With this approach to writing CVs you are almost guaranteed to get an interview.

Your CV needs to be customisable for each company and job that you go for. And the best way of doing this is to rewrite the profile whenever you apply for a job. So the first port of call is to create a generic profile and then we will look at how you customise it.

Writing the generic element of your profile is very easy. Let's just start with the list of skills that apply to the role that you're going for. All you need do is take that list of skills and write them into a couple of short sentences, perhaps a couple of paragraphs and connect them to the job you want to get. Let's look at two examples.

Here is a profile for an in-house training position:

> I am a highly skilled and qualified training and coaching specialist with a broad range of experience in training strategy, implementation, design and delivery over a diverse range of subjects. I am focused on generating excellent bottom line results through the empowerment and development of individuals by blending experience from training consultancy, managing teams in a highly reactive and volatile customer service environment as well as traditional engineering and sales orientated industries. I assist the development of individuals and teams to maximise their potential and create their own lasting success through the use of psychological techniques such as NLP and Accelerated Learning.

This is quite a long profile and would need to be cut down a little depending on the specific job being applied for. For example if the job being applied for was for a management development trainer that had to focus on design and delivery for a bank you might change it to read:

> I am a highly skilled and qualified training specialist with a broad range of experience in design and delivery over a diverse range of management subjects. I am focused on generating excellent bottom line results through the empowerment and development of managers. Blending experience from managing teams in highly reactive and volatile customer service environments, I assist the development of management teams to maximise their potential and create their own lasting success through the use of psychological techniques such as NLP and Accelerated Learning.

You could then go through your key achievements making sure that the right words are also appearing in your key achievements.

Now let's say you research the company and they have their values written up on their website. Here are "five guiding principles" that I have looked up on the internet for one of the major banks, just to use as an example:

- **Winning together** – achieving collective and individual success
- **Best people** – developing talented colleagues to reach their full potential, to ensure Big Corporate Bank retains a leading position in the global financial services industry
- **Customer and client focus** – understanding customers and serving them brilliantly
- **Pioneering** – driving new ideas, adding diverse skills and improving operational excellence
- **Trusted** – acting with the highest integrity to retain the trust of customers, external stakeholders and colleagues.

I might then modify my profile to read:

I am a highly skilled and qualified training specialist with a broad range of experience in design and delivery of pioneering management programmes to achieve collective and individual success. I can be trusted to focus on generating excellent bottom line results through developing talented colleagues to reach their full potential. Blending experience from managing teams in a highly reactive and client focused environment I assist the development of management teams to reach their potential and create individual lasting success through the use of pioneering techniques such as NLP and Accelerated Learning.

At this point I am often met with a particular objection that I would like to deal with. Many people say, "But won't the recruiters notice that you have used the exact words from the job criteria and the company values?"

The short answer is that is exactly what I want them to do. I want them to stop dead in their tracks and look at the CV. They may not believe it is true, but at this point I don't care. This is because once they stop they will look through the rest of the first page. This means they are looking through your key achievements and those key achievements are written as supporting evidence to the wild and extravagant statements you made in your profile. The impact on the recruiter is calculated to drop you on the must interview pile right then and there.

Occasionally in interview an interviewer will point out that your CV seems to be littered with the exact words and phrases that are on the company website or the job advert… and this is the best result that you could ever hope for. If an interviewer ever says this, from that point forward you have increased your chances of getting the job by several hundred percent. I will explain why in the section about interview questions.

We are going to look at some examples of other profiles, but before we do so, take the time to go through the profiles above again and notice how we have modified and tailored it, first for a specific job and then even further to fit the company values.

A worked example of developing a profile

Here is another profile I have taken from a CV on the internet:

> A motivated, adaptable and responsible graduate seeking an entry-level position in public relations which will utilise the organisational and communication skills developed through my involvement with *Student Magazine* and promotional work during vacations.
>
> During my degree I successfully combined my studies with work and other commitments showing myself to be self-motivated, organised and capable of working under pressure. I have a clear, logical mind with a practical approach to problem solving and a drive to see things through to completion. I enjoy working on my own initiative or in a team. In short, I am reliable, trustworthy, hardworking and eager to learn and have a genuine interest in PR.

I don't totally like this profile because it spends some time explaining how this person wants a job in PR and justifying her skills. Aside from that, this is not a bad place to start customising. So let us see if we can spruce it up a little.

Here is an entry level PR job I found from a recruitment site on the internet:

- **Company:** A National Charity who deal with a developmental disability.
- **Role:** The role will be working with the PR team to coordinate evidence to underpin PR activities, liaising with professional colleagues within the charity and outside. Responsibilities will include writing PR materials (with guidance), writing briefings on PR activities for internal and external audiences, helping organise PR events, updating PR information on the website, dealing with high volumes of telephone, written and email enquiries, organising mailings of PR material and providing general administrative support to the team.
- **Candidate:** The ideal candidate will be a graduate with experience in a charity press office or other PR environment. You will also have excellent communication and IT skills and have an interest in the media and press.

Based on this job, here is my version of the modified profile:

I am a highly motivated graduate with great interpersonal skills and a proven ability to work with teams. I have demonstrated a high degree of organisational skills through my PR work with *Student Magazine* and promotional work during vacations. I have a clear, logical and practical approach which allows me to complete large volumes of work in a high pressure environment. As a powerful communicator I am equally comfortable using written, telephone and email channels to make sure the right message goes to the right person.

As this job advertisement came from a recruitment company we may not be able to go any further in terms of customisation. But I would do a few internet searches. Firstly I would try to find the company itself; if not I would look at a few developmental disability charities and see if I could find some common phrases, values or buzz words.

From on a couple of sites I can get a feel for words like "dedicated", "professional" and the phrase "achieving their potential" has popped up more than once. Normally I would spend an hour or so researching this but let us assume we found these three were fairly commonplace in developmental disability charities. These words would now get popped into the profile. Here is one potential version.

I am a highly motivated graduate with great interpersonal skills and a proven ability to work with teams. I have demonstrated a high degree of organisational skills through my PR work with *Student Magazine* and promotional work during vacations, making sure that each project is achieving its potential. I have a clear, logical and professional approach which allows me to complete large volumes of work in a high pressure environment. As a powerful communicator I am dedicated to ensuring the right message goes to the right person whether in written, telephone or email form.

I would spend some more time honing this profile and I am sure that you have now got the idea of how to develop your profile and then customise it for a role, adding in the company values.

Here are three more generic profiles just to give you an idea of different styles and approaches:

Student looking for their first job in a call centre

Ambitious and enterprising student with a proven ability to learn fast and a commitment to getting quality results. Great communication skills, experience of working under pressure and to tight deadlines are key skills that I expect to use in my first commercial role.

Corporate Executive looking for bigger challenge

Random Name is an international bi-lingual executive with over 20 years experience overseeing European and USA operations. Having provided expert advice at board level for rapid growth companies, Random is a highly accomplished strategist with a track record of implementing key initiatives that have increased profits over various business sectors. Most recently Random Name has successfully overseen the buyout of Mega Corp International from Blue Chip Heaven and operated as a senior executive for Seriously Big Company.

Tech Projects Guy looking for a management role

I am highly qualified in (list most impressive tech areas) and have blended strong theoretical knowledge with cutting edge practical experience. I have a unique result orientated approach using key communication and negotiating strategies to drive projects to completion by building motivated teams of professionals.

Putting it all together

Here are a couple of profiles and the start of their professional experience so you can see how impactful this approach to CVs and résumés can be.

30-something professional looking for a better role

Profile

Versatile and analytic case officer with a practical hands on approach. Key skills of defining complex technical issues through accurate analysis of huge amounts of data, as well as excellent problem solving and negotiation skills, has led to a proven record of high quality, effective solutions.

Professional Experience

02/06 to Present
Senior Technical Case Officer Investigations Company

Main Duties

Investigating technical cases for cost and efficiency savings

Key Achievements

- Promoted twice in one year
- Developed investigations process leading to £1M saving p.a. for the company.
- Trained eight officers in advanced investigations techniques saving the company the external training consultant fees

---

**Returning-to-work mother after 10 year break
to raise children resuming a sales career**

Profile

I am a highly organised and energetic sales professional with experience of negotiating complex deals in a wide variety of areas. Using well developed communications skills combined with a results focused attitude I have a proven track record of exceeding sales targets as well as motivating teams to do the same.

1998 to Present

Raising Family

Key Achievements

- Successfully negotiated with schools and councils to get my children into the school of my choice
- Managed a fund raising event collecting £7,000 for a local charity
- Within two months of joining the PTA I was elected to the Exec Committee
- Negotiated nursery school fees down by 50%

In the final chapter on CVs we will deal with the second page, some of the frequently asked questions about CVs and finish off the application stage. But before you move on, put together your profile along with your professional experience in a generic way. Practise modifying them based on a company and see how it feels.

As a final exercise, just to make sure you realise how much more powerful your CV is than the standard, go and have a look on the internet at some of the CVs that are printed there as well as the advice some well meaning companies give you about how to put a CV together.

Writing Your Winning CV or Résumé Part Three: FAQs

I n the previous two chapters we have covered the critical aspects of your CV or résumé and in this chapter we will deal with the rest as well as handling some questions I am frequently asked.

The key point I would like you to remain aware of throughout the process is that the focus is not about you. It is all about the company and the role. You can see in the previous two chapters how we have applied that by modifying your experience to fit the role and the company. One place people seem to fall over in this approach is page two of their CV. So let us look at this in a little detail.

Page two

Page two is where you keep all the things that are expected of a CV but have no real bearing on the application. The question I am sometimes asked here is, if it has no bearing then why bother?

The answer is that in some situations it is entirely appropriate to only have a one page CV. In fact résumés are often condensed down to one page and contain only information that relates directly to the job. I am in favour of this approach and would also add in the UK the expected norm is two pages and a few accepted headings. To buck this trend may make your CV less palatable to an organisation.

Employers tend to be risk adverse when recruiting. The way to deal with this is to make your CV look normal but much better than the norm. Sending in a CV that breaks the boundaries will generally backfire. The caveat I will put on this is you need to match the expectations of the industry and the company you are applying to. Let me explain through a couple of examples.

A colleague of mine was looking for a job in PR and Marketing. One approach he tried was sending his CV on the back of a picture. The picture was of a couple of cute kittens playing underneath a ten ton weight that is held up by a rope and there is a hand with a knife just about to cut the rope. The caption read something like "Give me a job or the kittens get it". This approach got him several interviews. This was a great approach for his industry.

Years ago, when I was researching job hunting techniques, I drew up a few CVs as mind maps. I sent a mind map CV and a covering letter explaining how to read the mind map. I did this for two different types of jobs.

I was offered interviews when applying for trainer positions, though not as often as with a normal CV, but in each case when I was offered an interview they were very impressed with the bold, innovative approach.

When I used the same approach for an engineering position this approach failed spectacularly. I was not offered any interviews despite several times submitting a CV that matched the job spec completely.

In the first case I am still matched with the industry expectations but only just. In the second I had completely broken the boundaries and it didn't matter how good my CV was; because of its presentation I was not going to get an interview.

Therefore, if your particular industry expects a second

page with information that is not relevant then you should give it to them. If it is not necessary or expected, feel free to have a single sheet that has the relevant information on. In all circumstances, though, make sure everything that is relevant is on the front page.

The usual sections you find on page two are things like Education, Training Courses, Personal Interests and References. My tendency is to give enough information to make these things feel complete but nothing more than just enough. This is because it is easy to accidentally trip yourself up.

For example, putting on your CV the fact that you are an avid supporter of a local football team could cause problems if the recruiter reading the CV supports a rival team. I am not suggesting that all recruiters are unprofessional, although some might be. I am suggesting that on an unconscious level this recruiter might have notched up a bad mark against you without realising it themselves.

In terms of Education, unless it is relevant to the role (in which case it should appear on the front page), the older you get the less relevant this is. A rough rule of thumb is, compress the bits that are not relevant and expand the bits that are.

If you are in your 40s with a long and impressive career profile it would be appropriate to condense your education to a brief mention of several O Level/GCSE and A levels exams. If you are 18 and looking for your first, full time job you may have to expand the education section, even listing key achievements and specific course work to beef up your experience.

Until specifically asked, I would not supply referee details. And I would certainly never put their contact details on a CV. The most you should have on your CV is a line that says, References supplied on request.

Personal interests

Speaking as a recruiter I don't care that you have a black belt in origami and that you love your pet dog Snuffles. I only really care whether your face fits and you can do the job. With this in mind, don't go overboard with your personal interests. All you need are a couple of things that can be used as conversation openers to make you and the interviewer comfortable before the interview. And ideally these should be a couple of things you can work round to demonstrating key skills for the job you are applying for.

Big lists of your favourite TV programmes, books and restaurants are out unless there is some relevance.

Getting the important stuff onto the front page

We have talked earlier about putting the relevant section at the front of your CV and breaking it down into key achievements in exactly the same way you have been doing with your career profile. But let us take the more awkward example of having relevant experience, but it comes from several years ago and you have changed jobs several times.

There are two ways of approaching this situation. The first is to write your CV in a non chronological way. This means that you place the relevant experience first, relegating everything else to the second page. On the second page you put a brief chronological list. The expectation is that the recruiter sees the relevant details as you want them to but they can put it together chronologically later if they need to.

The second approach is my favoured one, but can sometime be difficult to achieve. All you do is be very brief with the non relevant details compressing them as much as possible to leave space for the relevant experience.

For example let's say you have had four retail jobs recently, you are going for a job as a programmer and five jobs ago you had some programming experience. I would compress the four recent jobs into one section, perhaps highlighting a couple of key achievements and then expand the fifth, more relevant experience. It might look something like this:

June 2008 to Present

Various Retail Positions Several Companies

Main Duties

Serving customers in various industries including hardware stores, supermarket and butchers

Key Achievements

- £2,000 worth of sales in a day when the daily average was set at £300
- Implemented new commuter stock control programme saving 40 staff hours per week

January 2006 to June 2008

Junior Programmer The Computer Company

Main Duties

Writing AI computer programmes to control non player characters in role playing games

Key Achievements

- Lots of bullets
- All relating to the job you are going for
- Making sure that it looks much bigger than the bits above

Consistency

One aspect that recruiters scan for is consistency. This can be an issue when following dates chronologically. I am in favour of making sure that there is an obvious chronological link right from your school days through your entire career, including any career breaks, all the way to your present circumstance.

Any breaks in that chronology are easy to spot and if you can't account for them you are raising the suspicions of the recruiter. It might be entirely innocent, but you are opening a loop and almost guaranteeing that it will come up in interview (or even worse they won't bring it up, but keep their suspicions).

For most people this is an easy task: just scan your CV and make sure all the chronological links are there and obvious. It only becomes an issue when you actually have something you would rather hide.

Earlier we talked about how you can generate key achievements from travelling, being unemployed, having a career break or raising a family. In which case you put them on your CV and display them proudly, linking them as achievements that mean you are ideal for the role you are going for.

But let's talk about worst case scenarios. Perhaps you suffered a complete mental break down and spent a year in a psychiatric hospital or you got caught robbing that bank and have spent several years in prison.

If you have these sorts of circumstances, I would not label them directly on your CV. Whilst in many cases it is illegal to discriminate, it is very easy to find an excuse to put your CV on the discard pile. My simple approach is to list the dates and place in the title the phrase, "To Be Discussed In Interview".

If you can get a couple of Key Achievements that don't give the game away then feel free to list them, but it is ok to leave them out if it makes it obvious what the gap was for. The reality is this is not a good situation, but doing this leaves you with an opportunity where as filling the space in could easily invite rejection.

By the time you get to interview you will have prepared what you are going to say and how you are going to reframe the situation so it appears in a good light. Or even more simply you get an opportunity to explain your side.

The one thing you must not do is leave a hole in your CV. Here is why. Most recruiters will check the time line so you can assume they will have spotted the hole and they will be suspicious. When you get to interview and the subject comes up, you are faced with not only framing the prejudice about the negative event, you also need to get over the suspicions of the interviewer and the idea that you tried to conceal it.

As a final note, if you do have something like this in your life there is tremendous pressure to conceal it with a lie. As I stated at the beginning of this book, you should never lie in the job hunting process. Even in this situation, it would be a complete disaster to lie for several reasons. The biggest is that, in the UK at least, lying on a CV could be classed as a criminal offence and you don't need to have got the job for the offence to be complete.

But let's say that you get the job through a lie. You then have to spend the rest of your time in that organisation hoping that lie does not come out. This will inevitably undermine your self esteem and confidence in the job.

Also consider what happens if that lie is discovered. In the worst case the company could call in the police and you could be prosecuted. More likely you will just be sacked and you are back on the job market with another event that you will have to reframe in interview. But perhaps they keep you on. If that happens what do you think will happen to your credibility and standing in the organisation.

It may be very tempting to lie, but please don't do it. Just spend the time and energy getting to the point where you can frame everything in your experience as a positive benefit to the role you are going for.

My CV is five pages long

If you have been doing the exercises and filling in your CV as we have been going along then I would expect this to currently be the case. And that is perfect. Everyone should keep a generic CV that you constantly update and tinker with.

When you find a job you would like to apply for, you will get the focus to chop that five pages down to two. You will have to make critical decisions about which elements of your CV are the most appropriate for that particular role, company or circumstance.

I would rather you have far too much information and have to prune really hard to get to the perfect CV. So if you have four or five pages of key achievements and relevant experiences then you are in the perfect place.

Application forms

Many companies and recruitment agencies are starting to use applications forms. And even worse they often say that they will not accept CVs attached to the form. The reality is application forms are a pain because you have to fill them in, but they are great for getting interviews.

An application form will ask specific questions. You can answer them in two ways. The first is obviously just transferring the information across from your CV making sure the key achievements are prominent.

Often on applications forms, though, they ask questions like, "Tell us in 500 words or less why you think you would be good at the job". With any of these sorts of questions you answer them using the hypnotic answer formula that you would use to answer an interview question. The only difference being that you are writing it down rather than speaking it. Obviously you will need to read up on the section about perfect interview answers, but once you have done so you will realise just how easy these questions are and what a great opportunity they are.

The sort of questions asked on application forms are golden nuggets that give you the opportunity to give great answers. So instead of being annoyed about having to do extra work when you have spent so much time creating a great CV, just remember the company has given you the ideal opportunity to demonstrate why you are the perfect candidate.

Covering letters

The final thing that we need to cover with CVs is the covering letter. Whenever sending a CV you need to attach a covering letter or email with it. There are just a few points you need to put in a covering letter to make it work well for you.

The key points you need to cover are the job you are applying for, including any reference numbers and where you found the advert. After this you just need to briefly outline why you think you are a good candidate for the position and link the job spec/advert to the experience on your CV.

Obviously, you also answer any questions that they ask in the advert. An example of this is the company asking a question like, "Why do you want to work for us?" And with this sort of thing you just use the hypnotic interview formula again.

An example covering email might look something like this:

Subject: Application for Pensions System Analyst/ Implementation Specialist

Hi John,

I am applying for the above position as detailed on your website yesterday. Please find my CV attached to this email.

As you will note from my CV, I am ideally suited to the position. You mention in the advertisement that you would like the candidate to have a strong working knowledge of the pensions system. I have held my current position for five years having worked extensively in various aspects of pension implementation.

In your advertisement you mention that the ideal candidate should be autonomous and creative. As you can see from my CV, whilst working for Pensions R Us one of my key achievements was single handedly adding an extra 20% ROI by implementing specific pension provisions. My manager of the time commented that this was the most creative solution she had seen in her entire career. I would gladly go through the details with you on interview.

I think I make a good candidate for this position and look forward to discussing this further with you in interview.

Warm Regards

Note the language in the last line. In NLP/Hypnosis jargon this is a future pace. We are presupposing that there will be an interview where certain things will be discussed. You want these covering letters to be this bold.

When you get a job advert that lists skills and attributes, you might consider in the covering letter cutting and pasting their list into a table. One column could be the job spec whilst the other would be the links on your CV highlighting the evidence that you meet the spec.

You now have a winning CV full of trance words, you know how to approach a covering letter and an application form. By using these ideas you will dramatically increase the number of interviews you will get. So in the next chapter we will look at interview preparation.

Developing A
Winning Attitude

I f you have been following the previous chapters and have developed your CV along the lines that I've suggested you will start to get lots of interview invitations. The next step is all about how you can ace those interviews. Over the next few chapters we're going to discuss an awful lot of sexy new ideas you can use in those interviews.

This particular chapter is all about the bedrock of how you're going to conduct yourself in those interviews. This chapter will deal with developing the attitude of the perfect interview candidate. We will also discuss how you can develop the confidence to act in this way and some neat tricks about keeping focused on the interview.

You might be a very confident person and therefore not feel the need for this chapter. I would urge you to read it nonetheless, because the issue isn't just about developing confidence it is about developing the right attitude to get you the job.

What is confidence?

Often people talk about confidence as if it were a thing. I prefer to think of confidence as a process which leads to a feeling. In fact I actually prefer to think of confidence as a process that leads to the absence of a feeling. To explain further what I mean, when we have removed all the emotional blocks, the negative thought patterns and the fear of failure, what we are left with is confidence.

Let me give you an example. In a few minutes I'm going to stop writing, walk out of the office and make a cup of tea. I'm going to do these things because that's what I've decided to do. And if I don't do them I will do something else. I am not emotionally attached, I have no fear of failure and I am happy that whatever result comes it will be a good one, although my expectation is that everything will happen the way that I want it to.

I don't need to psych myself up, set any goals or leap up and down to build my confidence. For me this is true confidence. It is all about the absence of any negative feelings, negative emotional attachments or fear of the consequences of not succeeding. In short the consequences of not making a cup of tea are not huge. This is the same attitude I would expect you to have walking into an interview.

When you walk into an interview your body will be preparing you for an important situation. It will be releasing chemicals into your bloodstream that make you more alert and more focused. It will be trying to tell you that this is important and you should be paying attention. If you are not going to interviews with these sorts of feelings I would suggest that you are being complacent. Many people can confuse these feelings as being nervous. They are not the same thing.

So in summary I would expect you to be walking into an interview being focused and alert but comfortable in your ability to give a good account of yourself. Whether the company has the good sense to employ you or not is of no consequence. The reality is, if you have done all the right things with your CV you will be offered lots of job interviews so not being offered any one job has little or no consequence. The rest of this chapter is about how you develop that attitude.

Dealing with the blocks

Let's start with some of the typical blocks and negative beliefs that people often have about job selection and interviews. Then we can start looking at the reality, or at least the attitude that you could develop to blow these out the water.

"I don't deserve this job/I'm not good enough"

If you truly don't deserve it then why are you applying for it? You should be walking in with an attitude of "I am going to be great for this company and this job, do they deserve me?"

Using the system from this book, you will be getting lots more job interviews and as a result be offered more jobs. Therefore I think you have a responsibility to only apply for jobs that you can do really well in companies you really want to work for. What this means is you are actually doing the company a favour by applying for the job and they should be demonstrating to you all the reasons why you should take their job.

"I'm being tested."

Actually the reality is that you are giving the company the opportunity to see the greatness of you and how much benefit they will get by employing you. You are also testing the company to see if they are a good fit for what you want.

You want to be walking into the interview with the attitude of offering the company an opportunity. They have this one chance to see what an ideal candidate you are and if they fail to capitalise on it that is their problem.

"I really want this job."

It may be a really good job in a really good company but there are thousands of jobs and thousands of companies. With the system in this book you will get more and more opportunities. Getting emotionally attached to any one position is exactly the thing that will potentially stop you getting the job. Think about this analogy: have you ever met a desperate salesman? My guess is if you've ever met one of these, even if the product was good for you, chances are that you didn't buy.

It may take you a few goes with applying this system before you realise how much power you gain from it. Several people that I know personally have applied this approach several times over, rapidly moving into jobs in positions that they want. Once you recognise this for yourself, you will quickly come to the conclusion that no one job is worth worrying about.

"I am not prepared."

Well the reality here is perhaps you should have prepared. And once you've been through the whole book and understood how easy it is to formulate answers to interview questions you will always be more prepared than most job seeking chumps. Once you are comfortable with the system it will take you minutes if not seconds to prepare yourself. Obviously researching the company is a different matter but even without that will be able to give a really good account of yourself. I should state, though, I am an advocate of good preparation.

In short, you should only be applying for jobs that you know are good for you and in which you can give the company a good return on their investment. You deserve this sort of role, to be treated with dignity, respect and to be paid what you are worth to the company. Using the system outlined in this book will open up a multitude of those opportunities.

As you start to meet all these criteria you might start to recognise that you are giving the company an opportunity to find out how good you are and what a great return of investment you would be. Whilst it is your responsibility to make it easy for them to see this opportunity, if they fail to grasp the situation there are no major consequences for you as there are plenty more jobs and companies out there.

Developing the attitude

In this section we are going to look at an exercise to develop a great winning attitude for going in to job interviews. Let's start by defining that attitude in positive terms. Here are a few statements that I think are useful in demonstrating a good winning attitude:

- I have selected this job and company because I will be good for them and they will be good for me
- I want to give this company the opportunity to see how much benefit I would be for them
- There are lots of jobs for me to choose from, this one is no more important than any of the others
- I am testing them to make sure this is an organisation I would be proud to work for
- I am going to have fun in this interview and just see how much I can excite the interviewer with how good a candidate I am

These are just a few statements that I think are valuable. You might want to spend a few moments thinking about and adding to this list. If you don't think of any more that is ok, because this is good enough to start with.

We are now going to do an exercise to start developing this attitude. First let me start by letting you into a secret. People don't really sit down and give you statements about their attitude to things. It just leaks out through their behaviour. What they do, what they say and how they say it all give you clues about their attitude.

This is just as well because we don't really want to walk into an interview and say these statements to an interviewer. That would be a bit strange. What we want to do is let this attitude leak out through our behaviour in the interview.

On a connected note, remember one of the things we are looking to do is appear different from the rest of the candidates, but not so different that it breaks the usual interview convention. Developing this attitude and letting it seep out through your behaviour will make you a little different from the norm.

Here is the exercise. I suggest that you read it through in full, so you understand what is going on, and then just follow the steps. The exercise is about first visualising how someone with this attitude would act and then starting to feel what it would be like to act that way. In the next section we will see how to use these images to create a way of dealing with interview nerves and staying focused.

Some people don't recognise that they make pictures in their heads. In fact a small minority of people make pictures and then take them away so fast that they don't realise that they are making pictures. If you fall into that category then this exercise will work just as well for you. When we take about visualisation just imagine that you can make the pictures in your head and follow along imagining the scenes and situations.

If you are more comfortable focusing on the words, the feelings or the sounds instead of the pictures then that is a fantastic way of doing this. In fact the more senses you can use the better this will work. If you are the sort of person that talks to yourself in your head, just become the narrator for this exercise as if it were a radio play.

You brain visualises better when you are relaxed. Take a few moments to imagine someone, real, fictitious or purely imaginary, who has the attitude we have been discussing. Imagine them walking into a company and doing an interview. What you are looking for are the behaviours that display this attitude. Here are some of the things I can imagine:

- This person would talk in a slightly lower and slower voice (this is typical of confident, relaxed people).

- This person would sit and stand straight whilst still looking relaxed

- They would smile, make eye contact and use their hands to gesture whilst they speak.

- They would ask questions as well as answer them and the interview would feel much more like a conversation

Those are some ideas I thought of, but this is your exercise so you create the behaviour of this imaginary person for yourself. You might want to think about:

- How they would sit, stand, walk and talk

- How and what they say in answer to questions

- How they demonstrate their personality and confidence

- What they believe about themselves and their world

The key is being able to see their behaviour and notice the impact this has on the interviewer.

At this stage you might be thinking I don't have enough details to get all this right, I don't know how to give a perfect answer, I don't know which company or job I am actually going for and so on. That is ok because I am going to ask you to do this exercise many times.

Each time you gain more information I would like

Dissacoca'Aion -then Association

you to do this exercise again, adding in the new material. When you learn the perfect interview answer you can add that to this exercise; you can do it again when you learn about how to deal with awkward questions. When you have an interview confirmed with a specific company you can do the exercise again using their company name.

Repetition is a great way of installing habits, so doing this exercise several times is highly recommended and certainly when you have more information to add it is critical.

Take your time imagining this situation and replay it several times getting the details and this imaginary person's behaviour exactly right.

Now that you have run through the interview watching this imaginary person doing a brilliant job, the next step is to start at the beginning of the interview again. But this time, before they go into the scene, morph the features of this imaginary person into your features. So now you are watching yourself going through this interview. Remember to get everything right, just like you did as the imaginary person.

Start from the beginning of the interview again. This time, before starting the situation, just float down into your imaginary body. This time explore the perfect interview from behind your own eyes. So instead of looking at yourself in the picture, imagine seeing out through those imaginary eyes, seeing what you would be seeing, hearing what you would be hearing and feeling what you would be feeling as you go through the perfect interview.

If you have a need to understand what is going on here, I am taking you through a modelling process; this is what NLP is about. The process is very simple. You start by imagining someone else having a perfect interview. It is easier to be objective about someone else's performance.

Once you have got this imagination right we are changing the features so it looks like you. This is the start of getting your brain to accept doing things in this way. Finally you float down into the body and imagine what it would feel like to act in this kind of way yourself. You get to feel what acting in the way that you want to act would be like. The more often you go through this process, the more comfortable the new behaviour will feel.

There is one extra note I should add to this. Some people spend a huge number of hours visualising success. In fact I know a few that spend so much time doing these exercises that they have little time to actually make a success of their lives. Your brain works really fast and much faster than reality so this should be a quick exercise and certainly take you no more than ten or 15 minutes.

As you go through this book you will gain more information about what you could add into your visualisations. The benefit is in the detail so you might want to do this exercise several times just concentrating on the first part of an interview, or dealing with some of the difficult questions, or a perfect hypnotic future pace. It is ok and also good for you to break the interview into sections and do this exercise around those specific sections, but also imagine the complete interview so you can experience all the parts flowing together as a whole.

Also note that repetition is a great way of installing new habits. So you will get much more benefit from doing this exercise for ten minutes each day for six days than you would doing this as a hour long exercise.

Finally, this is the inside of *your* head, so do the exercise in the way that has most meaning for you) Also, don't let your mind take control. I have met some people with such low self esteem that they seem to be able to imagine the worst things happening to them. Recognise that you are in control of your mind. These exercises are for your benefit so take charge of your mind and imagine the situations you need for you to get the benefit from them.

Once you have done this exercise a few times it will become second nature for you. We are going to use some of this visualisation as a way of dealing with interview nerves and maintaining your focus, so it is important that you get a good foundation in doing this exercise.

Dealing with nerves

We are going to look at a couple of ways of controlling nerves, should they come up. If you have read the rest of this chapter and done the exercise above you will have dealt with most of the issues that cause nerves, but there are a couple of things worth noting that will then completely blow the issue away.

Earlier in this chapter, we discussed the fact that it can be easy to confuse the signals from your body. When your body is preparing for an important event it floods chemicals into your brain that make you more alert and focused. These feelings can easily be misinterpreted as nerves. We are going to do a little exercise so you can tell the difference between them and change your interpretation of the feelings from being nervous to being focused.

Think of something that makes you nervous. Please pick something that just creates a little bit of anxiety, not a complete mental breakdown. This is an exercise in exploring the feelings of nerves, not an exercise in sending you into a psychiatric ward.

Most people will notice that the feeling of nerves is created along the centre line of the body and somewhere between the stomach and the chest. They will also notice that the feeling starts low and builds in intensity. However you experience the feeling is fine and that is what we will use. Take hold of the feeling and move it a couple of inches higher in the body. Then move it a few inches below the original position. You will start to notice that it is easy to move along the centreline and that moving it in one or both directions actually diminishes the feeling.

Just moving the feeling changes it. Just practice thinking about interviews and if you get any nervous feelings, simply move them to where you can still feel alert and focused but have let go of the nerves.

Peripheral vision / INSTANT DE-STRESSOR

The final technique I am going to show you is about your peripheral vision. This is a very powerful technique that has huge benefits beyond dealing with your nerves, but we will restrict ourselves to how to use this for interview situations.

Your peripheral vision is linked to your nervous system. When you are relaxed you tend to have a wider field of view; when you are stressed your vision tends to draw in to a single point of focus. You know this instinctively to be true. Think about times you have been stressed and recognise that tunnel vision is part of your stress response.

Knowing this about the way that your body works, by deliberately going further into peripheral vision will bring out a relaxation response. Let's give you a real experience of this happening through another exercise.

Developing A Winning Attitude

Pick a spot on the wall opposite you just above eye level. Look at the spot; don't stare, just look. Whilst looking at the spot notice that you can see other things in the room; perhaps the corners of the room, the ceiling and the floor, as well as other people or features of the room. Whilst remaining focused on the spot widen out your vision and notice all the other things in the room. Your peripheral vision is great at noticing colour and movement but does not do detail particularly well.

Notice that doing this starts making your body more relaxed. The thing most people notice first is that it goes quiet inside your head and feels a little like being in a daydream. You can help this feeling even further by taking a few deep breaths and unclenching your jaw. Now, keep hold of the feeling, move your eyes back down and start looking around the room.

When you first do this it might be a little disorientating. But after a few minutes practice it will feel quite normal. Whilst in peripheral vision, try and get nervous and notice that you can't. Because of the way your vision and nervous system are connected, the only way you can properly start experiencing nerves is to start tunnelling your vision.

Now you have experienced the benefits of peripheral vision, we are going to use this to build a system for staying relaxed and focused in the interview. Here is what I would like you to practise.

Sit down. Go into a nice, relaxed state and imagine a spot on the wall slightly above eye level. In that spot imagine all the feelings of confidence that you have ever experienced. Picture all those times you have been at the top of your game and getting great results. Make sure you really feel it as you put this visualisation into that spot on the wall.

RE- READ THIS PAGE FOR DIFFERENT APPS ?

SALES /ANY TYPE OF MEETING!!

Remember all the visualisation you have been creating to develop your interview attitude? You can now put all of those in the spot on the wall as well. Now take your eyes away from the spot for a moment.

When you are ready look at the spot, take a deep breath in, let it go whilst accessing all the feelings you put into the spot and at the same time just go into peripheral vision. Notice the feeling you access when you do this. Bring your eyes back down keeping hold of the relaxed, focussed and confident feeling.

Practise a few times looking at the spot, taking a deep breath and releasing it whilst accessing the feelings and going into peripheral vision, then bringing your eyes back to your normal eye level whilst keeping hold of the feeling. After a few goes it becomes an automatic process and happens so quickly that no one else would notice.

I hope you have already recognised what a powerful result you can get from this. Now you have created this spot and, as obviously it is only in your mind, you can pick it up and take it anywhere you want. You could, for example, imagine this spot in the interview room just above your normal eye line and be able to look at it any time you want.

You could, for example, go through your relaxation process when you enter the room before anything has started. Suppose you suddenly start feeling nervous just as the interview begins. Instantly, you can go through your process again and stay calm. Let us say the interview is going well when suddenly the interviewer drops a bombshell that you were not expecting and it knocks you off your game. No problem, you just look at your spot, go through your process then ask the interviewer to repeat the question to give you time to formulate your ideal answer.

In this chapter we have discussed how to develop a great attitude towards the interview, looked at dropping the blocks to confidence and how to deal with nerves. In the next chapter I will show you how you can win the interview in the first two minutes as well as take covert control of the whole process. Between now and then, spend a few minutes a day over the next week developing the attitude and practicing peripheral vision.

The First Two Minutes

V arious research studies that have been done on interviews suggest that interviewers make all their decisions in the first two minutes. The rest of the interview is used to find the evidence to support their decision. The implication for us is that if we can get the first two minutes right everything else will flow. With that in mind, this chapter is dedicated to the first two minutes of the interview.

By the end of this chapter you will know what you should do when you get to the company, how to take covert control of the process before you have even stepped into the room and elicited the interviewer's personal values.

Before the first two minutes

There are a few things you might want to consider before getting to the interview. The key issue about job hunting is attitude. If you get that right everything else flows a lot better. So the night before an interview spend some time making sure you are prepared.

The night before, make sure you find the time to get relaxed, go into peripheral vision and visualise the whole interview process from arriving at the company, through the first two minutes and practise you interview answers.

One of the things that scupper interview candidates is failing to come across as believable. To counter this you might want to take along a folder or portfolio of your key achievements. If you are in sales and have performed well perhaps you might want to take your last three months of sales figures. You might want to take along letters of compliments, your last appraisal, academic certificates or anything that shows you in a good light. Ideally you should have examples and interview answers prepared which allow you to use these documents as evidence.

If you take this approach, though, remember presentation. It does not matter how good the evidence is if it is presented on a screwed up piece of paper that has spent the last ten years in your back pocket. Invest in a decent briefcase and a portfolio or folder to keep these documents nicely presented. A really nice touch is to have all of these as a copy and leave it with the interviewer at the end.

Make sure you know how to get to the company and leave enough time to get there about half an hour early. Don't go in, though, until about 10 minutes before you are due. This makes you look like a whizz at time management. Spend the time getting your state right, go into peripheral vision to take the edge off any nerves and visualise the whole interview again.

Ok, now we are ready to talk about the first two minutes.

Building authority, credibility and rapport

Your first task, before the interview has started, is to build authority, credibility and rapport. This is actually simple to do. In fact it is easier to do than to explain how to do it. I want you to understand the concept behind how to do this so you can modify the approach to suit you and your circumstances. So, we will start by looking at some theory first and then move into how you can apply the approach specifically to interview situations.

For NLP jargon junkies, we will be talking about rapport, pacing and leading. (People like people that are like themselves.) Think about the people who you are close to and you will notice that you have a lot of things in common. You might like the same things, but you might also notice that you tend to talk the same way, use certain words and hold various common beliefs.

This matching can also be noticed on a non-verbal level. Think about a specific event in the past when you were with a person you are very close to. As you remember back to that event, notice that at the time you seemed to match or mirror the other person's body language, their tone and pace of speaking. Spend a few minutes people-watching in a café or bar and you will see this happening a lot.

Matching and mirroring is an indicator of rapport. Some NLPers incorrectly suggest that rapport comes from matching and mirroring body language. This can work, but it is a very inefficient way of trying to build rapport and we will look at something a little more powerful below.

The other thing you will notice when you spend time people-watching is that there is usually a rapport leader. In groups one person will often move – for example lean into the conversation – and the other people will, within a few seconds, follow the behaviour. This all normally happens outside people's conscious awareness, but what it means is that the rapport leader is, on a non-verbal level, taking complete control of the situation and the others are following.

From our perspective, if you had a process that took covert control of the situation you would automatically build authority, credibility and rapport with your interviewer. This is the process we will build below.

103

Big and beaming, how to pace and lead your interviewer

I am going to show you a process that will allow you to pace and lead the interview situation right from the start. In jargon-free terms this means that you build rapport and on a non-verbal level actually take control of the situation.

Before we start talking about the actual process, I need you to do a thought experiment with me. Just follow along with the exercise I suggest below, and afterwards I will show you how it is important in terms of the process you use to get control of the interview.

Imagine you are walking down your local high street and in the distance you can see a person approaching. From a distance they looked vaguely familiar, but as they get closer they start looking like a very dear friend that you have not seen for a very long time. At first you are not quite sure that it is them, and even still you start remembering all the good times that you've had with this person. You start to smile, hesitantly at first, then as the person gets closer you realise it really is them and you rush forward excitedly to greet them.

I want you to reread the last paragraph with a view to what happens to your internal feelings and your non-verbal signals as you imagine the situation. If you are like most people, what you will sense on the inside is a slow but steady build up of warm friendship and excitement. You will also probably notice that you will have a smile that starts off slow and hesitant but eventually winds up being big and beaming. If you are strongly imagining the situation you can probably see yourself going to shake the hand of this friend or hug and kiss them depending on how you treat your friends.

BEFORE / DURING every MEETING.

Persuasion Skills Black Book of Job Hunting Techniques

You may be wondering what this has got to do with your interview. The reality is, I want you to go through in your mind this exact process as you meet your interviewer. From the outside it will look like a small, hesitant smile that grows into a big and beaming friendly, warm greeting as you reach out your hand to shake theirs. In a moment I will explain exactly why this works very powerfully but there is one thing I want to clear up first.

It is vitally important that you follow the process and that you imagine the interviewer is a long lost friend. This is because it is extremely difficult to fake non-verbal signals. Everyone picks up on these non-verbal signals, but not necessarily consciously. In simpler terms, you can't fake a warm friendly greeting. In fact you may well have had the experience. Compare times when you have met up with people you genuinely care for and times where you have had to meet someone who you know is neutral towards or dislikes you. With experience, you know you can tell the difference between genuine warmth and someone faking it. This is why it is important to get into the mindset of going through a slow and hesitant smile that grows into big and beaming in a very genuine way.

In a moment we will discuss how you can practise this approach until it is instinctive, but first let me explain why this works. The things you think about inside affect how you react and in our particular situation they have a strong impact on your non-verbal signals. By imagining that you are just about to meet and greet a long lost friend you are making yourself feel good, relaxed and this is reflected in your non-verbal signals.

We have been socialised to respond to particular signals. One particular signal that works very powerfully is smiling. It is almost impossible not to smile back at someone who smiles at you. But what we respond to most strongly is not someone is smiling at us but someone who goes from a neutral face to smiling widely.

So if you approach your interviewer grinning widely like a lunatic it will not work. But if you approach them with a neutral face slightly hesitant and grow a genuine smile they will feel good and they will smile back at you. Notice what is happening here, your interviewer is following your lead and is feeling good about doing it.

The next thing that you do is walk up to them and put your hand out to shake theirs. This is another non-verbal signal that we are socialised to respond to. When you put your hand out as if to shake someone's hand, it produces an almost automatic response from the other person to take your hand and return the handshake. Again, you have made a gesture and your interviewer is responding to it. In one fell swoop you have started leading and the interviewer is following you – and feeling good about it.

Using this process you have, in the first few seconds of meeting your interviewer, given them a very powerful signal that you have authority, can lead and are also very likeable. You have also managed to look different from most interview candidates. Most interview candidates are giving off nervous non-verbal signals and are looking to the interviewer to lead the situation.

The only thing that remains is to discuss how you are going to practise this. The reality is it needs little or no practice, just do it. Make a point over the next few days of, whenever you meet someone, going through the whole big and beaming process. It doesn't matter whether it's people you know, have never met before or are even members of your family. Just do it and notice their reactions. If you are really brave, stand on a street corner and meet random strangers. You will be really surprised at the brilliant reaction that you get.

Let me explain how powerful this processes is. A few years ago a friend of mine, Trev, was going for a job interview as a store manager. I didn't know that he was going for a job until a couple of nights before when I met him for a drink. Trev told me that there were certain holes in his CV and in his interview technique and was asking for my help. Unfortunately, it was too late to do very much.

I was thinking of how I could help my mate in the short time that we had when I suddenly realised that the biggest issue is the first two minutes. And so all I taught him was how to smile and shake hands in the way that I have shown you above. In fact it was Trev who came up with the phrase "big and beaming". I had Trev practising in the pub that night and for the next couple of days. He now uses it as an automatic process for meeting anyone and is scarily popular.

On the day of the interview Trev arrived at the store 10 minutes early. This is something I would recommend to everyone. Trev then lit up a cigarette and stood outside the store. This is something that I would not recommend to anyone, but he did it anyway. As he was smoking his cigarette, a man came up to go into the store. Since I had had Trev practising this big and beaming process for the last two days, he automatically used it on the guy walking into the store. They stopped for a few minutes and chatted and then the guy went in.

As you've probably guessed, this guy was one of Trev's interviewers. Later Trev told me this was one of the most schizophrenic interviews he has ever had. This is because the guy that he had met outside was talking to Trev as if he were actually already working for the company. The second interviewer, according to Trev, clearly was concerned about some of the gaps in his experience. In fact, Trev was of the opinion that if it had been left to the other interviewer he would not have got the job.

Now that we have looked at taking control from a non-verbal perspective, let us look at maintaining this and getting the key information you want to feedback in interview.

Eliciting your interviewer's personal trance words

Before getting into the interview, there is usually some chat. Interviewers do this to settle themselves down as well as settle the interviewee and get them talking. This is all good stuff and gives you some great opportunities.

The first thing I would suggest is that you start to ask questions. Typically there is some light conversation before the interview and you will find interviewer and interviewee flapping their gums at each other about the weather, transport systems and how easy the company is to find. In this situation I would start to ask questions about the interviewer, giving them the opportunity to talk about themselves.

By being genuinely interested in the interviewer you will be giving them some good vibes, come across as more confident and different from the standard interview candidate. This all creates a great impression and allows you to keep covert control of the situation. But there is a more important reason for doing this.

There is one great question that you should ask and keep asking of your interviewer. The question is, "What is important to you about (x)?" The (x) is any relevant context you can get into the conversation. Here are a few examples:

- What is important to you about your role?
- What is important to you about working for this company?
- What is important to you about the people you hire?
- What is important to you about the people that you work with?

Notice, particularly with the last two questions, what sort of information you are likely to get back.

When you ask the "what is important to you?" question, you are getting some very powerful information from people about their motivation in a particular context) In fact you are getting some of the person's personal trance words. What I mean by this is that these answers have a deep rooted psychological impact on them. Let's look at how this can work for you in an interview.

Imagine you manage to ask my most favourite of these questions, ||What is important to you about the people you work with?|| And you get an answer back like, "I like working with people who are really creative at problem solving and focused on getting the work done." Guess what you will be saying to this interviewer when the interview starts.

Here is an answer to a "difficult" interview question like "Tell me about yourself". You might formulate an answer that starts, "Rather than tell you everything about myself, I will just focus on some of my key skills. I am a creative problem solver and focused on getting the work done. For example, when working for XYZ Company when I did…" As you can see, this answer feeds into the interviewer's personal trance words.

Let's take another question such as, "What's important to you about working for this company?"

Perhaps the response you get back might be something like, "I enjoy working for a large company where there are great career opportunities."

When in the interview you get asked a question like "Why did you apply to work here?" or "What do you want to get from working in this company?" or "Why do you want to leave your current employment?" you will want to respond with something like, "I want to work in a company large enough to offer great career opportunities to the people that prove themselves. I have a commitment to any company that I work for to be extremely effective, for example two months ago when I..."

Again we are feeding back the interviewer's personal trance words. Don't worry about the structure of these responses and how you are supposed to come up with them. You will be spouting these in your sleep when you have been through the next couple of chapters. All I want you to recognise is that you are feeding these personal trance words back to the interviewer.

The thing I often get asked at this point is, "Don't interviewers notice?" Most of the time the interviewers don't know that you're doing this. And actually it's a great result when they do notice. This approach is exactly the same as what you are doing with your CV when you do your research on the company website. In that case what you are doing is finding the personal trance words of the company by looking at their website. In this case you'll find the trance words of the interviewer by simply asking them. In either case you want them to actually notice the fact that you are feeding back their trance words. This is because you can have a really great killer answer ready for them. We will talk more about this issue over the next couple of chapters.

The only challenge about using these kind of tactics is to disguise the question as part of a conversation. Remember, when you first meet your interviewer you want to open up a conversation and ask some questions. You will take covert control of the situation, as we discussed above, and then initiate a conversation. Somewhere in the middle of this conversation you will ask the question, "what is important to you about...?" which can be about any context you like, but the best ones would be work, the company, the people you work with the people you hire, or your team (this is really good if you are talking to the person who would be your direct line manager). And then your feed those personal trance words back to the interviewer during the interview process.

Here is a typical line of conversation and a way you can turn things round to ask the question. Imagine turning up for the interview and after your flash of big and beaming the interviewer says something like:

Interviewer: "Glad you are here, did you find us alright?"
You: "I did thank you, it is quite an easy place to find, do you live locally or do you travel in?"

Notice what is happening here, you have responded to the question and then asked one of your own. It doesn't matter how the interviewer responds, all you will do is link to their response and then ask another question. Here is how the conversation might play out.

Interviewer: "I live locally and have done for many years."

You: "It must be great not having to travel for hours to get to work. Have you worked for the company long?

Interviewer: "I have been here for three years doing (blah, blah…deleted for brevity)."

You: "It sounds like you really enjoy your job, what is important to you about your job?"

Interviewer: "I just love problem solving, working with lots of different people and having fun. I think it is important that people have fun at work as well."
You: "I guess fun and people are important too. What is important to you about the people that you work with?"

Interviewer: "I like the people here because they are open, trustworthy and like having fun."

You: "Seems like a great place to work, if I were successful would you be my manager?"

And so on whilst you walk to the interview room. This is a made up conversation and I hope you can already see it is easy to hide the key questions in a conversation.

There are a few points worth noting in this conversation. Firstly, notice that the question was asked in context and was linked to the conversation. This makes it part of the conversation. Also, notice the fact that the question was asked twice for two different contexts. So long as it is part of the conversation and sounds normal, you can keep asking this question over and over.

The reason for asking twice is that by the second time we had got to the best context. Also, we got a really powerful extra here. Notice that the interviewer repeated the word "fun" in both sets of values. This is an indicator that this is a very important personal trance word for them and therefore is a real biggy to drop into your interview answers.

We have to deal with the issue of not getting nice, clean answers like the demonstration above. Nine times out of ten you will get some good answers to feed back. If you are unfortunate and they give you stock rather than personal answers, or there is a distraction and the topic of conversation changes, just let it go. Every little helps and it is great to get a person's personal trance words, but if you don't achieve this every time it is ok; you have plenty more opportunities.

If you work in a company and are going for a job switch or promotion, then this process is much easier. Before the interview, in fact preferably before you have sent in your CV, phone up the manager for the new role and ask them for a tour of the department, to discuss the role etc. And as part of that opportunity, or even during the phone, call just ask the question.

Finally, asking this question in a conversation is easy and it becomes easier as well as automatic, if you practise it. Most of the time the issue is not in asking the question, but properly hearing, remembering and feeding back the responses a little later. This is also very easy once you have practised a little. So make a commitment to yourself to spend a few minutes the next time you have a conversation to ask the question and feed back their response a few minutes later as part of the conversation. The context is not important, the practice is. Here is an example:

Random Person: "...So I stayed in last night and just caught up with my favourite programmes."

You: "It's good to get some down time, so what were you watching?

RP: "Just *Eastenders* and a film."

You: "You like *Eastenders*. What's important to you about that show?"

RP: "I like the depressing characters and plots, makes me feel better about life."

You: "I get the idea it makes you feel good about working here, is that what you like about films as well?

RP: "No, with films I prefer action adventure films."

You: "Really, what's important to you about action adventures?"

I think you get the idea. What you might also practice is remembering their values and just working them back into a conversation ten minutes later.

As a final note, when you turn up for the interview do this process with everyone you meet. When I was working as a training manager I had occasion to interview people for training positions. Whilst my PA was not part of the formal interview process he certainly expressed a view on many of the candidates. I remember one occasion when I was borderline on whether to employ a particular candidate. The thing that made me decide not to take them on was my PA grumbling about how stand-offish this particular candidate had been prior to the interview. My argument was that the person would be working as part of a team and would be working with my PA. If they could create such a bad impression in such a short space of time then they were lacking in some of the key skills that I needed for the role. This may not have been fair, but I would suggest this sort of thing happens all the time.

Putting it all together

Before leaving this chapter I want us to return to the original issue. Research suggests that interviewers make their minds up within the first two minutes and spend the rest of their time gathering the evidence to support that decision. By really focusing on getting the first two minutes right, the rest of the interview will matter less.

In this chapter you have learnt how to take covert control of the situation, create a conversation and bring out the personal trance words of the interviewer. Doing all of this right will leap your chances of getting the job through the roof.

Before going into the sexy bit about developing hypnotic answers to any interview question, let us pause for breath and look at putting all we have learnt into a process.

- Start with getting the attitude of "I'm good and I'm going to give a great return of investment on any job I choose to hold. I am going to give a company the opportunity to recognise just how valuable I will be for them."
- Put together a killer CV or résumé with lots of key achievements and a profile that links directly to your job criteria.
- Do some basic research on the company you are applying to and populate your CV or résumé with company values, buzz and trance words.
- Put together a grab bag of evidence of some of your greatest achievement in a nice portfolio or folder. Make sure you include a couple of copies of the right CV.
- The night before, run through the whole

interview, make sure you have your examples sorted out and you can answer any interview question (dealt with in the next three chapters).

- Turn up to the interview half an hour early but don't go in until ten minutes before the appointed time. Spend the time getting into a great state, use peripheral vision to take the edge off your nerves and picture yourself going through the process giving great answers.

NB

- When you do walk into the building do the big and beaming process with everyone you meet, especially the receptionist.

- When you meet your interviewer, do big and beaming, take covert control and start asking questions. Elicit their personal trance words and remember them so you can bring them out in the interview.

If you get all of this exactly right, you probably won't need the next few chapters about great interview answers and dealing with difficult questions. But just to be on the safe side we will cover a basic formula that allows you to answer almost any interview questions with ease and then devote an entire chapter to the worst questions you could ever be asked as well as how you can turn them into golden nuggets of opportunities.

Basic Answer Formula

O ver the next three chapters we are going to look at how you can answer any interview question confidently. The issue isn't the confidence with which you answer the questions but how much you can sell yourself with those answers.

Many people get very stressed about interviews and it all seems to centre around the questions that they are asked. You can buy books of interview questions with ideal interview answers in them. I think this is a complete red herring.

Imagine a situation where you have a book of 500 interview questions and perfect answers for each one of them. The first issue comes is that those answers may seem to be ideal, but if they don't fit your experience and they are not in the context of the job and the company, how can they be ideal? You could go through the whole of the book modifying all the answers to fit your situation. Assuming you've managed to do all that work then you would need to memorise them all and be quick witted enough to remember the right answer to the questions that you are asked in the interview.

Imagine a different situation; imagine that you have a formula for the perfect interview question and it works 99% of the time. Imagine that you have the confidence to know that your formula works in any situation and that you have practised that formula until it is almost instinctive. That is the position that you will find yourself in as you work through the next three chapters.

In this chapter we are just going to outline the

anatomy of the good hypnotic answer. In the next chapter we will look at be taking that framework and fitting it to your exact circumstances. After that we will look at those difficult questions and situations and how you can still fit your basic formula around them.

The anatomy of a good hypnotic answer

There are several things that we want to make sure your answers give the interviewer. Remember, the whole job hunting thing is not about you, it is about how you fit into the role in the company. All of your answers need to reflect the fact that you can provide massive benefit to the company and that you were born for the role.

BEING BELIEVABLE

Research suggests that interview candidates are not inherently believable in interview. The issue has been compounded by the fact that there have been a lot of complaints and high profile cases of people lying on their CVs. Your interview answers should put interviewers at their ease because they appear believable.

Take this the right way: I expect you to be entirely honest in the job hunting process. There are loads of jobs you can go for and you can fit your experience to reflect most of them. If there is no way you can fit your experience to the job you want then you shouldn't be applying for that job. What you should be doing is applying for the job that will give you the experience to get the job you want.

Just because an interview candidate is being entirely honest it doesn't mean that they come across as believable. Most of the time it is not that the interviewer consciously disbelieves the candidate it is just that the interviewer is left with some sort of nagging doubt.

Again, when you look at the research the reasons are simple and the solution is very straightforward. What many interview candidates fail to do is give enough detail in their answers. Let me explain by way of example. Here is a typical interview question: "What key skill will you bring to the role?" Consider these two answers:

- "I am very task focused and I'm exceptionally good at getting the job done. It doesn't matter what happens around me I will get the task done regardless."

- "One of the key skills I would bring to the role is being very task focused when needed. For example, last year on June 23 my department went into meltdown. We missed several key deadlines and it looked like we would lose a lot of money. Amongst all the chaos I realised that there were four key tasks that needed doing and if we did them we could minimise the impact of missing the deadlines. Despite all the noise and confusion, the shouting and screaming I got the job done and saved the department. This is how focused I will be at getting the job done when I come to work for you. I have with me the letter of thanks I was given by the CEO of the company here with me if you would like to see it."

Obviously the situation is hypothetical and I've just made it up for the purposes of this example but I hope it demonstrates the difference between an interview answer and a believable interview answer.

Our interview answers will be built on concrete examples and will ideally be backed up with any other evidence you can provide. Remember, way back when you were putting your CV together, I was asking you to think of key experiences you can turn into achievements on your CV. One of the reasons for taking that approach is it increases your believability factor if your interviewer has already seen something about the experiences you talk about in an interview.

The absolutely perfect situation would be a key achievement on your CV which is then discussed in interview and you brought along documentary evidence to the interview to back up your statements. Obviously this is not always achievable and I recommend that you search hard through your experience to find one of these. If you can find one, the benefits are unbelievable.

ACKNOWLEDGING, AGREEING, PACING THEN LEADING

Hypnotists and NLPers use a technique called "pacing and leading". In simple terms the idea is that if you are first given statements that are true for you or that you agree with, you are more likely to agree with the statements that follow.

Here is how a hypnotist might use this idea. When taking someone into trance, they might say something like, "As I speak, you are sitting in the chair listening to my voice and becoming more relaxed." During this statement from the hypnotist, the client is sitting in a chair listening to the hypnotist's voice. All of these are facts that the client can verify. The final statement "...becoming more relaxed" is not necessarily true, but the hypnotist is hoping to get the client to do this. The client is more likely to take this suggestion on because of the three verifiable facts That have been stated first.

You can find the same sort of techniques in sales. In sales the technique is called "building a yes set". A sales professional will ask you a series of questions all of which you can only answer yes. They are hoping that you will say yes to the last question which is usually a buying decision.

Have a look at the two interview answers above. You will notice that the first answer just starts, whilst the second answer acknowledges the question by repeating back the key phrases and then builds the answer from it.

There are several reasons for doing this. Firstly, it shows that you understand the question and it gives you time to formulate your response. But the key reason for responding in this way is because it builds agreement and paces your interviewer.

I wouldn't necessarily do this for every answer, but by having a few acknowledgement, agreement and pacing statements to put in front of your answers you will gain another little edge in making sure the interviewer really takes on board your answers.

BENEFIT STATEMENTS

This is another little bit of standard sales training. A good sales professional is actually focused more on the customer than anything else. They may have a great product with lots of features but that does not mean anything to the customer. What the customer wants to know is how they will benefit from the features that the product has.

Remember, an interview is not about you, it's about the benefits you will provide the company when they employ you. With this in mind it makes sense to talk about the benefits the company will get. You may think that it is the interviewer's job to draw this out of you. I personally would rather take charge and make sure the interviewer really knows the benefits of employing you.

Notice in the second interview answer above, the candidate very specifically says that they will be focused and get the job done. This happens at the end of them detailing a specific experience where they had done just that. Some people think that this is an overstatement; the reality is that you are making sure that the interviewer makes the connections. Think about it this way: the interviewer has just asked about one of your key skills and all you have done is answer that question and then connect it to how the company can specifically benefit.

Your ideal interview answer will start by acknowledging and linking what the interviewer said to a specific piece of experience you have had. You will then join the dots for the interviewer by connecting your experience to key skills, qualities or attributes they need for the role and then tell them the benefits that the company will gain. In the next chapter you will discover how to do this.

How To Answer Any Interview Question

In the last chapter we looked at some of the component parts of a perfect interview answer. In this chapter we are going to get into more detail and I'm going to show you exactly how to put together a great interview answer. If you follow through with the exercises by the end of this chapter you will have enough material to confidently go for two or three hours of interview questioning.

You could use what you will learn in the next couple of chapters to answer every question, including something like, "Would you like a cup of tea?" The issue is not that you use this formula for every single question but that you are walking in with the confidence of knowing that you have prepared answers that you can use for every conceivable question. So if you find a question that you have a better answer for than any of the ones that you have prepared, then go for it. But if nothing comes to mind that is better than what you have prepared already, use the information in the next two chapters because these answers are powerful.

Before we get into the detail, I want to give you an example of exactly how powerful this system can be. I should mention that I do not recommend doing any of what I am just about to tell you. This situation came about because I was researching how to do interviews – what was effective and how to create the perfect interview answer.

As part of the research that I was doing I needed to get to lots of different types of interviews and try out many different varieties of techniques in live conditions. As a result I used lots of different CVs and applied for a huge variety of roles. My intention was never to take any of the roles under false pretences. I was purely doing research.

Whilst in this research phase, I was once offered a technical management role worth £60,000 per annum after I had told the interviewers that I totally lied on my CV and that I had none of the experience or qualifications that they were asking for. Much of the reason that I got offered this job has to do with all of the things that we've talked about in previous chapters. Certainly the only reason I was interviewed was because of the CV that I had sent in.

The CV was entirely false, it was actually my mate's CV that I had adopted and made my own. None of the experience or qualifications that were on the CV was mine. In fact in some places the CV was so technical I had no idea of what it actually meant.

I was called for interview on the basis of that CV. When I arrived I went through all of the pacing and leading and rapport techniques that we have discussed in previous chapters. I was interviewed by two people, the head of department who would be my direct manager and a HR executive. I got on brilliantly with both of them until the start of the interview. The HR executive explained the he would be asking more of the general questions and the Head of Department would be asking some technical questions based on my experience and qualifications.

At this point I thought the game was up and I started telling them that the CV was fake. Obviously this caused a certain amount of confusion and they asked me why I had applied for a job with a fake CV.

I obviously hadn't planned this, but they gave me the opportunity to use the interview formula that we are going to look at below. The answer I gave them astounded them, in fact it astounded me. As a result they interviewed me for about 45 minutes; they asked me back a couple of days later, interviewed me again and then offered me the job. Obviously I was researching interview techniques and the like and for that reason alone it would not have been right for me to accept the position, but for a while I was sorely tempted. I think I had even talked myself into wanting to do the role.

I want to reiterate the fact that I sent in a fake CV, got caught out and basically told my interviewers that I had none of the experience or qualifications that they had asked for. Despite this they still offered me the job. The reason they did this was because I gave them such a phenomenal answer to the question of why I applied for a job that I had no experience or qualifications for. In this section I am going to show you how you can create those phenomenal answers but using your actual experience from your CV.

In this chapter we will build up the process for creating excellent interview answers. There is a basic formula that once you have assimilated, will allow you to answer almost any interview question. In fact even those difficult and awkward questions can be answered using this basic formula; we are going to put in interesting little tweaks to deal with the awkward bits.

It is important that you work through this chapter and do the exercises. If you do this and practise a little, you will be answering interview-type questions instinctively, almost without having to think about it. I think you will agree this is a much more useful skill than memorising hundreds of generic good answers to generic interview questions.

To accompany this book you can download my PDF report which has over 500 interview questions. When you've got your interview formula in place you can check it against all of these questions and notice that you can instinctively come up with answers to all of them. This should give you enough confidence to recognise that you can answer any interview question with the system that I am about to give you.

Using your experience

As we have discussed in the previous chapter, you will already recognise that detailing your experience is what makes you more believable. There are several reasons for this: by filling in facts and figures in detail you sound believable; because you'll be recounting your experiences you can add your passion, interest and all the details that come with real experience. The great thing is you can use almost any experience to come up with a great interview answer. Let me prove this to you.

Let's take four typical interview questions, choose an experience and see if we can formulate some good interview answers from it. Here are three typical interview questions that I picked randomly:

- "Give me an example of your communication skills." This is an evidence-based question.

- "What unique experience separates you from the other candidates?" This is one of the top 15 most frequently asked questions.

- "Tell me about yourself." This question is in the top 10 of most disliked interview questions.

We are going to take a random piece of experience and see if we can build good interview answers to these questions. This is despite the experience being a little silly. We will then do the exercise again with a better experience and you can see that this approach works with almost any piece of experience.

For the first piece of experience I am going to select the fact that I got up this morning, but only just, and I didn't manage to make it into my office until 11 o'clock. So let's see how we can answer that first question using this experience.

A good example of my communication skills would have been this morning when I didn't manage to get in to the office until 11 o'clock. I was feeling tired and lethargic and very unmotivated, but by using my communication skills I talked myself into getting into the office and doing some great work. Normally we talk about communication skills with others but often the way that we talk to ourselves in our heads makes a big difference. The benefit to you is that if I can demonstrate these motivational skills on myself under difficult circumstances I will be really good at motivating my team in your company.

As you can see this is not a great piece of experience to use for this particular question, but notice that despite this we can still get a reasonable answer to the question.

Let's try this again with the same experience but with question two.

I have lots of unique abilities and one specific experience that separates me from all of your other candidates is having the focus and the flexibility to be able to get the job done. For example this morning I didn't get into the office until 11 o'clock. This is because I was feeling tired and needed a lie in. When I awoke this morning I worked out exactly what needed doing in the office today and how long it would take me. Knowing that afforded me the time to get an extra couple of hours sleep. This meant I got into the office refreshed, excited and motivated and got everything that needed doing done. When working for you I will apply the same logical reasoning to make sure that everything gets done on time with the least amount of stress to me and my team.

I hope you're starting to see how one bizarre little piece of experience can be used to demonstrate many different things. Let's look at that third question.

There are many different things I can tell you about myself and I would like to focus on some core skills for the job. The job I'm applying for requires focus and flexibility. These are skills that I have in abundance, for example this morning I didn't get into work until 11 o'clock. I didn't come in until late because I wanted an extra couple of hours sleep and knew that I would be better focused on getting everything done if I had it. I had the flexibility to take a couple of hours off and the focus to still get the job done. When working for you I will have the flexibility to deal with unexpected circumstances and the focus to still get the job done.

I hope my point is made, a piece of experience that you would never want to bring up in interview and I can still use it for some good interview answers. We will look at some case studies and examples with better pieces of experience later in the chapter.

What I want you to notice at this time is that the answers to the questions all follow that basic formula you learnt in the previous chapter. They all pace the question that was asked, they all have a detailed piece of evidence and they all have a benefit statement that connects that experience to usefulness in the company.

Just for the practice of thinking in this way, take some of your experiences and use them to answer those three questions using this basic formula. I would also suggest that you answer out loud. There is a big difference between thinking things through in your head and actually saying them. Your perfect practice opportunity is if you can get someone else to feed you the questions and you answer them. Failing that, sit in front of a mirror, imagine someone asking you a question and watch yourself as you give the answers. If you don't have a mirror that you can practise with, still say the answers out loud. Trust me, this sort of practice will pay you back dividends. As we develop your answers I will be asking you to do this again with your real experiences.

Gathering your experience

When I was researching how to succeed at interviews I once went to an interview with just one piece of evidence. I was determined to use this one piece of evidence for every question I was asked. I would like to say that I got the job, but unfortunately I didn't. I must have come across very strangely in the interview – almost as if there was only ever one incident that had ever happened in my life. But for me the interview was a success because I did manage to answer every single question with only one piece of evidence.

Obviously you are not researching, you just want the job. Having sat through hundreds of interviews from both sides of the desk as well as coaching hundreds more, I know that if you have five pieces of evidence you can cover several hours of the most exacting interviews.

Remember, earlier on you were gathering evidence to use for key achievements for your CV. Now is the time to bring your CV out again look back through those key achievements and find the five achievements that you are going to use as the bedrock of your interview.

You are obviously looking for the biggest, greatest and most impressive of your achievements that fit the role you are going for. Ideally it would be best if you can have separate documentary evidence of each of these achievements. You also want to check that you can link these experiences to the key skills and experiences that are required for the type of job that you're going after. For example if you are going for a job as an underwater basket weaver you might want to select experiences that demonstrate nimble fingers, holding your breath and being able to function underwater.

If you are coming up with experiences that are not on your CV ask yourself why they are not on your CV. If they are that good and relate directly to the job you are applying for then perhaps they should be.

Once you have selected your five pieces of experience your next job is to be able to explain them in three different ways. The first way is a short thirty second sound bite. It should be very brief and in this formula:

On a particular date I did (x) resulting in (y)

Here is an example:

On May 2005, with only one evening's notice, I was asked to run a two day personal development programme for 200 sales advisors. Despite no preparation time I delivered a course that had feedback like "This was the best two days training I have had in any company I have ever worked for".

This version of explaining your experience is based on opening a loop. You give the interviewer the situation and then the result you created without much about how you did it. You are using this with an expectation that the interviewer will ask how you achieved the result and then you can give them more detail. You will only use this short answer version for those situations where the longer answers do not seem appropriate. For example, if you are using the same piece of evidence for a second or third time.

The second way is a slightly longer formula and is the standard that you will normally use when answering questions.

The standard interview answer should follow the STAR Formula. STAR stands for:

- Situation or Task
- Action you took
- Results you achieved

Here is an example:

Back in May 2005 I was working as a training consultant and had been asked to do some consultancy work with a call centre. The evening I arrived at the hotel I was met by one of the Directors and asked if I would help them out by taking over 200 staff that they had employed and keep them occupied for two days as there had been a delay in getting the new systems ready. I agreed to deliver a two day personal development seminar for them starting the next morning. The rest of that evening I questioned the director to get an insight into the people, what would benefit them and drew up some plans of things I knew I could deliver that would be effective. The result from the two days was great. Many of the 200 delegates wrote feedback forms saying this was the most enjoyable and effective course they have ever been on.

The third way of answering is just a longer, more detailed version of the second. The important thing is that it should be **relevant** detail. So in the example above I would not say any more about how the situation came about. But I might add a lot more about the questions I asked the director, the design of the course, elements about the delivery or more information about the feedback and results that were achieved. This third, longer answer is only for use when you are specifically asked to go into more detail.

You would rarely give the third answer in full. Usually you might give a little bit of it to add, clarify or answer a point when questioned. The idea in practising the long third version is to make sure that you have the relevant details in mind and can articulate them in a meaningful form.

You now have some work to do. Gather your five experiences and any documentary evidence to support them. Work them round to three different versions of each as above and practise saying them out loud. You might think you can skip the out loud bit, but please do this. Once you have had a go at speaking them out loud you will recognise just how different this feels when practising and what a significant improvement it will make when you get to your interview.

Pacing and linking statements

Now that you have a range of experiences to work with, let's start looking at how you are going to link them to the questions that you are asked. Here are a few generic interview questions:

- Tell me about a time when you demonstrated (insert key job skill e.g. decision making)
- Describe your ideal job
- What do you know about our company?
- Why are you interested in this position?
- Talk me through your CV
- What sort of a manager are you?
- What is your biggest development area and what have you learned from it?

I'm going to use that example of delivering training to 200 people to show you how I can link it to all of these

132

questions. At the front of this book is a web address where you can download free bonuses that complement material in this book. Included in that bonus material is a PDF manual of over 500 interview questions. I highly recommend that you not only download the manual but you also practice linking your five experiences to the questions that you will read there. After you have done a little bit of pacing and linking it will become instinctive to you. The following examples should give you a good idea of how to do this.

Tell me about a time when you demonstrated (insert key job skill e.g. Decision-making)

"Decision-making is critical to the role as I see it and I'm a good decision-maker in a high pressure environment. For example, in May 2005 I was asked to run a course for two days and 200 people with little or no notice. I could have said no, but I have the flexibility to think through difficult situations. I gave due consideration to the numbers of people, the fact I had no design time and that I had a lot of material in my head that could work. I also thought through a plan of how I could design the course as I went along. On a balance of probabilities it looked like this was achievable against the problems that would be caused if I did not do it. Based on all these factors I made a decision to run the course and the result was a great course with terrific feedback and results.

Describe your ideal job

My ideal job would include a combination of using some of my core skills as well as challenging me. I have great flexibility, love training and I thrive in high pressure environments. Combining these into a role would be ideal for me. An example of the sort of thing I mean is in May 2005 when I got the opportunity to deliver…

What do you know about our company?
I know something about your company as I have done some research. The research I've done seems to suggest that you are looking for people who can rise to the challenge and work flexibly on their own initiative especially in high pressure training environments. An example of where in I have done this would be May 2005 when I got the opportunity to deliver...

Why are you interested in this position?
I'm interested in this position because it will give me the opportunity to use some of my key skills. I have great flexibility, love training and I thrive in high pressure environments. I believe this role contains elements of each of these. An example of how I can thrive in these sorts of environment would be in May 2005...

Talk me through your CV
There are many ways I can talk you through my CV and I think the most useful for you is to focus on some of my core skills. You can see from various pieces of experience on my CV that I have great flexibility, love training and I thrive in high pressure environments. A really good example of this you can see my CV from May 2005 when I had the opportunity to...

What sort of a manager are you?
What sort of a manager am I? As a manager I have a huge amount of flexibility and thrive in high pressure environments. I am as happy managing small teams as I am managing large ones. A great example of my management skills occurred in May 2005 when I had the opportunity to deliver a two-day course for 200 people

with no design time. One of the key strategies I used to deliver this was building a small core team of helpers out of the 200 so that we could design the course as we went along. The course was an astounding success with great feedback and results. This occurred because I have the ability to not only manage my core team of four helpers but also the larger group of 200 people.

What is your biggest development area and what have you learned from it?

My biggest development area is being flexible enough to rise to any challenge however unreasonable. Whilst this is useful in high pressure environments to continually be this flexible I do not give the company the chance to improve. In May 2005 I had the opportunity to deliver a two-day course for 200 people with no notice. I rose to the challenge and delivered a great course. The issue for the company, though, is that knowing that I have that flexibility allows them to avoid taking the opportunity to change so that we don't create those sorts of situations. My key learning is to bring up these issues with the organisation whilst maintaining flexibility to deal with them as they arise.

As you can see from these examples, this piece of experience fits better with some questions than it does others. That is why you are choosing five pieces of experience to work with rather than just one. That said, I would like you to take your five pieces of experience and fit them into every conceivable question that you can think of. This is simply so that you get the practice of being able to think in this way.

Trust me that, if you take your five pieces of experience and make each piece of experience fit all of these seven questions, by the end of it you will really understand how to fit any experience to any question. Then it's just a matter of practice and pretty soon you will be doing it in your sleep. This is a great skill to develop because what we are now going to look at is how you can add some extra zing to these experiences by adding in corporate buzzwords, personal trance words and values.

Values statements

Remember that when we were putting your CV together we looked at researching the company. One of the key things we were looking for was the company values corporate buzzwords and hot buttons. We also looked at the job advert or spec. You used all of these in your CV, predominantly in your profile. You can use them all again in the interview. This is something that you can prepare the night before your interview.

Also, in the chapter about the first two minutes we discussed how you can elicit your interviewer's personal trance words. You can also use these in your interview. The only difficulty with the interviewer's personal trance words is that you have to do this in the moment. Let's have a look at how you might do this with the example that we had above.

Let's say that during your company research you found one of the company core values was flexibility and you also found on the job spec the phrase "high pressure training environment" repeated several times. Knowing this information, go back and reread the answers I gave you above.

Now let us say that in your conversation before the interview started your interviewer told you one of his personal trance words was fun. I am going to assume that you would find it easy to add the word fun into any one of those answers above. And for the sake of completeness here is the beginning of the first answer with added fun:

Decision-making is critical to the role as I see it. I'm a good decision-maker in a high pressure environment and have a lot of fun being able to use my skills in this way. For example in May 2005 I was asked to run a course for two days and 200 people with little or no notice…

Doing this obviously needs practice, but you would probably recognise that it's very easy once you start doing it. There are several things that you want to practise. The first is, now that you have all of your experiences together and you have started practising pacing and linking phrases, you could just look up some companies, find their values and trance words and practise integrating those into your interview answers. Obviously you will practise in a much more targeted way when you have some companies you are definitely applying for.

You can practice eliciting people's personal trance words in normal conversation. Somewhere in the conversation just ask the question, "What's important to you about (x)?" This is good practice because that is essentially what you're going to do to your interviewer.

Once you have found someone's personal trance words you can, a little while later in the conversation, work those words back in. This again is really good practice and is actually harder than what you're going to do in an interview. Remember, a conversation can go anywhere so you will have to think on your feet about how you work the question in and how you will feed the values back. In the interview all of your answers are prepared because you are using one of your five experiences. Therefore you already have the main bulk of the content ready, you just need to add your interviewer's personal trance words.

A final note on practising: thinking things through in your head and knowing how they work is great. But if you want it to work for you in interview then you need to practise out loud. The perfect practice would be to have someone reading out those questions to you randomly and you answering out loud. The next best thing would be for you to read through a question and answer out loud in front of the mirror. Even without a mirror to sit in front of, still answer the questions out loud.

Benefit statements and future pacing

All your answers need to end with either a benefit statement or a future pacing statement and ideally both. So let's have a look at what these things are and how you can put them into your answers.

For our purposes, a benefit statement is a statement that explains to the interviewer how they would benefit from you being in the company. If we go back to the examples that we were using above, a benefit statement would look like:

"…and that means I have the flexibility to rise to any challenge that your high pressure training environment can create."

As you can see from this statement, all I am doing is restating the core skill and telling the interviewer that it would be useful to have this skill in their company. Here is another version:

"…the benefits to you are that it does not matter what kind of situations your high pressure training environment creates, I have the flexibility to react to them."

A future pacing statement is a statement that forces the interviewer to imagine you already in the role. Let me explain a little further: to make sense of what I am saying you have to form a representation of it in your mind. For example if I were to say, "think about how good you will feel when you start your new job," you have to form an internal representation of this situation just to make sense of the sentence. It doesn't matter whether that internal representation is a picture of you doing the job or just a feeling or a sense of doing the job; it doesn't matter if you agree with the idea or not, but just to make sense of the sentence you have to form the internal representation. This is one of the ways that your mind works with language.

So consider the possibility of implanting in your interviewer's mind things like:

- you doing a fantastic job
- a great return on investment for employing you
- the interviewer's boss thanking them for hiring such a brilliant employee
- you making a great success in the company
- you do all the things that the interviewer imagines is possible for that particular role

I wouldn't use future pacing statements for all of your interview answers because it might sound a little odd; I would sprinkle them throughout your interview. Let's imagine for a moment that the interviewer in the previous examples would be your direct line manager. Based on that, here are a few future pace examples of how you can end your answer:

- "Imagine how much you could do with the department when you have this amount of flexibility in your team."
- "High pressure environments are always reactive. When we work together I have the flexibility to deal with this reactive environment whilst you can work on resolving the situations that create these problems."
- "...and what that means to you is that we have the flexibility to deal with these sorts of reactive situations. How often do you think we will have

to react in this sort of way?"

- "Consider the possibilities of having this amount of flexibility; how will this impact the way that you organise the team?"

I hope you're noticing that each of these statements is forcing the interviewer to think about you actually doing the job. These are either bold statements or questions and are not entirely normal in an interview situation. That means that you have to treat them with a little care but certainly get them into the interview because they are very powerful.

Future pace statements don't necessarily have to be at the end of the response to a question. I bring them in at this particular point because they have a great use at the end of your answers, but feel free to bring them in at any stage of the interview. There are some that would be good for the end of the interview, for example, "How do you see me fitting into the department?" Or, "What sort of career opportunities can you see opening up for me in your company over the next five years?"

If versus when

Consider these two different versions of a future pacing statement:

- "If I come and work for you, here are all the benefits that you will get…"
- "When I come and work for you, here are all the benefits that you will get…"

All things being equal, I would use "when" because this is the stronger of the two statements. If I was not as confident in the rapport that I had with the interviewer I probably use "if I come and work for you…"

These statements are bold and evocative, they are

extremely powerful and as such they should be used with care, but they should be used. Before we leave future pace statements, here is an email I received that describes a perfect way of using a future pace statement in an interview:

From: Eugene
Sent: 05 May 2010 03:38
To: Rintu Basu
Website: www.Seagriff.com
Subject: Interview pattern I used today

Hi Rintu

Thought you might want to share this with your students as evidence your book is priceless. Had an interview with the GM I would be reporting to this am – first face to face meeting after being screened carefully by a recruiting firm and a prior phone interview with him.

Of the several patterns I employed (including, "how do you imagine us working together, with you being based in Louisville and me in NY?"), this was my favorite:

"Once you've selected the candidate and they have been in the position for a while, how do you envision success? I mean – what will I be doing and achieving, how will I be interacting within the organization, you know – how does it look and feel when it's working?" You could literally see the wheels spinning as he thought about it for a while smiling slightly…

Shortly afterwards he said that the next step is for me to speak with his boss and he initiated a discussion to figure out the soonest opportunity for that to happen. I'll be sure to ask him the same question!

Thanks for the virtual help! And please be gratified to know that each time I read the book my understanding grows deeper (nearly through the second time now).

Eugene

Where are we now?

Many interview candidates have issues with the questions. They don't know what to say, they don't know how to prepare and some people can get themselves into a real mess trying to think about what they need to know for the interview.

Now consider where you are in terms of interviews. If you have been following along and doing the exercises you now have five pieces of experience, any one of which will answer 90% of questions that you're asked. These pieces of experience are linked to your CV and you also know how to modify them to fit directly with the company, the role and the interviewer. You have also practised making direct benefit statements and future pacing statements that link you to great results for the company. I think this pretty much makes you completely bullet-proof in the interview.

In the next chapter we are going to discuss some of those difficult or awkward questions. You are going to discover that some of the questions most interview candidates struggle with are golden nuggets of opportunity for you. I'm going to show you how you can redirect a low ball question into an opportunity for you to say great things about yourself. But the vast majority of the next chapter relies on the fact that you have got this basic answer formula well prepared. So put together your experiences and practise saying them to people and I will see you in the next chapter.

Dealing With Difficult Questions

In the last chapter you discovered how you can use your experiences to create the answers to almost any question. All you need is a linking phrase at the beginning and benefits or future pace at the end of your answer. We also learnt that if you have rehearsed and practised five key experiences they should be enough for many hours of interview. You then worked out how you can add personal trance words, corporate buzzwords and any other hot buttons that you can push into your answers.

Having prepared in this way you should have a huge amount of confidence about what goes on in the interview. In essence, you will take covert control of the interview from the moment you walk in to the moment you walk out. In NLP training we tend to think of the person asking the questions as the person in control of the conversation. Whilst this is generally true, by using the system outlined in this book what you have done is very subtly shift the balance of power. This is because it doesn't matter what questions you are asked, you have a rock solid, prepared answer.

That said, there is always the opportunity for the interviewer to take you off your stride by asking a low ball question. There are also situations where things come up in interview that you'd prefer not to have, where you have weaknesses or holes in your experience that you need to cover or, the worst possible set of circumstances, when the interviewer does something illegal or inappropriate. I aim to address all of these issues in this chapter.

But I just told you that

Before getting into the classic difficult questions, let's just deal with a common fear that people have when I outline the idea of using values and trance words. Firstly it is very rare that an interviewer will notice that you are using their personal trance words or even the company values on your CV.

If it does happen, here is how you should respond. Just pause, look at them a little confused and say something like, "Of course I am using your words; I care enough about this position that I want to communicate effectively with you. Don't all the candidates do this?"

If the question was about you putting all the company values on your CV, the response is something like, "Of course I linked the corporate values to my experiences; I am supposed to be demonstrating how I match the company. Aren't the company values important enough for you to check that the employees you hire reflect them?"

I'm sure those two examples are enough for you to figure a few more responses for yourself. The key point is that this should be normal job hunting behaviour and you might want to point out how the interviewer is benefitting from the approach. In fact if you want to be very smug you might want to add on a piece of experience about great communication skills, include their trance words, a corporate value and end in a benefit statement.

Classic difficult questions

Let's start with some of the questions traditionally thought of as quite difficult to answer. We will split these into several little categories.

WIDE OPEN QUESTIONS

There are some questions that people find difficult to answer because they are so wide and open. Here are some examples:

- "Tell me about yourself."
- "Talk me through your CV."
- "What would you bring to the company on the job?"

These questions are thought of as difficult because they're wide and you have to talk about yourself. In reality these questions are real golden nuggets and can give you the opportunity to win the job right then and there.

A few years ago I was working for a large corporate call centre. I was in the strange position where I was training interviewers to interview and I was training interviewees to pass interviews. For various reasons outside the scope of this book, I like training interviewers to start with wide open questions like the ones above. Obviously I was training my interviewees to respond to these questions in much the same way as I'm going to show you now.

On several occasions I had one of my interviewers come up and tell me that an interview candidates had almost completely passed all the criteria for the interview in the first five minutes with the answer to the very first question. That is how powerful this system is when it is applied to these open questions. So let's look at how you can answer these questions and almost ace the interview on your first question.

The answer to this question relies on the research that you've done on the company. Remember, before the interview – in fact when you were putting your CV together – you looked up all the company values and the core skills for the job. You also linked all these to the experiences that you were going to use in your interview. All of a sudden these wide open questions can be answered exceptionally easily. Let's take the "Tell me about yourself" question and look at how you can answer it.

"I can tell you a lot of things about myself and what I will do is focus on some of my core skills such as (lists several core skills that are related either to the company or specifically to the job). An example of where I clearly demonstrated these skills was on... (leading to your most favourite key experience and ending with massive benefit statements and a future pace.)"

I hope you already realise that the only thing you need is a decent linking phrase at the beginning and the rest just follows our standard answers. For the sake of completeness here are the linking phrases for some more of these sorts of questions.

- **Talk me through your CV**. "There are several ways of talking through my CV and what I will do is focus on some of my core skills..."

- **What would you bring to the job?** "There are lots of skills that I would bring to this job and what I will do is focus on some of my core skills..."

- **What do you look for in a job?** "For me to really enjoy the role I need the opportunity to be challenged and use my key skills, for example..."

- **Why do you want to come and work for us?**

"Having researched the company and the role, I believe you will give me the opportunity to use some of my core skills to their best, for example…"

This should give you enough of an idea of how to link these wide questions right back to the material you have already prepared. The key I want you to recognise is that when you get asked a question like this it is a great opportunity for you to shine and really show what you are worth.

NEGATIVE QUESTIONS

This next category of questions is one where the interviewer asks you to speak negatively about yourself. The most common of these is, "Tell me about your biggest mistake or failure." There are other versions such as, "What is your biggest weakness?" or "What skills do you need to develop further?"

Many interviewers ask these questions without actually understanding the purpose of them. The real question is, "Tell me about your biggest mistake and what you've learnt from it." Or, "What is your biggest weakness and how do you intend to develop in this area?" As you can see, the issue isn't what has happened, it is about what you've done about it.

There is one school of thought about answering these questions with a strength and making it seem like a weakness. I don't agree with this approach because it is not genuine and easy to see through. Any interviewer worth their salt will challenge this approach. My answer to this is to be open about any problem or weakness and tell the interviewer how you are intending to deal with it.

For most people, when they pick their five experiences they will have one example that fits this category. An example from the previous chapter is where we talked about delivering two days of training for 200 people at a moment's notice. You could use this example to illustrate a big risk, rash decision-making or something interesting such as giving into company demands when taking a different approach would have allowed the company to grow and develop.

If one of your experiences doesn't fit for creating this kind of answer, you will have to add on one more piece of experience. This experience can be anything where you have failed, made a mistake or just not performed the way that you should have. The key, though, is to go beyond the experience with something you have done to develop, learn or put in place to make sure you get different results the next time. Here are a few examples of the sort things that I mean:

A sales professional losing a big sale because they didn't present the product properly and now they make sure that they always present the product appropriately.

A manager who had to sack someone for poor performance now realising that they could have spotted the signs earlier and put development or corrective action in place to increase performance and save the person's job. The manager has now put together a checklist of early warning signs that may lead to poor performance that they can start correcting before it becomes a problem.

A trainer getting devastatingly poor feedback results on a course realising it was because they didn't motivate the delegates well enough at the beginning and now having a course structure that includes this motivational element.

Once you have this piece of experience you can use it just as you have any of the others in the previous chapter.

General objection handling

Before we move into the next type of questions, I want to spend a few moments explaining a particular phrase that allows you to redirect interviewer's thoughts. For the NLP jargon junkies, this phrase is called a redefine and it goes like this:

THE ISSUE ISN'T (X), THE ISSUE IS (Y)

You can use this phrase to redirect a question and can use it when you're interviewer asks dumb questions. Here are a few questions and how you can use this phrase to redirect them to something more useful.

Tell me why we shouldn't hire you.
"The issue isn't why you shouldn't hire me. The issue is what you will be missing by not hiring me. Let me tell you about my core skills and how they apply to your job. One of my core skills is... (and you're back to your general answer formula)"

Tell me why you want to leave your current position.
"The issue isn't why I want to leave my company. The issue is about me wanting to join your company. Let me tell you about why I am such a good fit into your company and into this role. One of my core skills is..."

How do you deal with bad management?
"The issue is not about bad management; it's about how I can remain effective whatever else is going on around me. Let me tell you about the core skills I use to be effective. One of my core skills is..."

This should give you enough of an idea as to how you can redirect any question back to focusing on the key issue, which is how you fit the company and the role.

Holes and weaknesses in your experience

If you have a hole in your CV or weakness in your experience, or you just don't completely match the job criteria you should know this in advance. And therefore you will come prepared for it. The first thing that you want to do is reframe the problem into something useful for the company. Let me give you an example:

A few years I helped a 19-year-old whom we will call David get a job in a large corporate bank. The job that he was applying for required a large amount of financial customer care experience and the average age of the people doing the job was mid to late 20s. We were fairly certain that this was an issue and therefore we needed to reframe the lack of experience and the fact that David was only 19.

Thinking this through, you could argue that not having the same experience as everyone else means that you will do things differently and potentially find new solutions to old problems. Being younger than most of the employees could mean more energy, drive and ambition. Both of these things can be a significant benefit to the company.

I had David practising the phrase below until he was saying in his sleep:

"One significant advantage that I can give your company is the fact that I'm younger and far less experienced than the rest of your employees. Do you want people that just routinely do things the same way that they've always done or do you want someone young, fresh and dynamic who can look at things in a different light? This is an area where I can give you a clear result, for example… (into a massive achievement that David had created for his last company and highlighted all of his key skills)"

David told me later that the interviewer actually did bring up his lack of experience. He told me that he responded with, "The issue isn't my lack of experience, but what great results I can give you because of it." He then went into the prepared example above. He said that his interviewer went into complete meltdown because it was a totally unexpected answer. David said that as he went through his example she was nodding away, smiling and agreeing with him. Needless to say, he got the job. We will never know, but I like to think that David got the job on the strength of this answer.

What you need to be aware of is that these particular types of issues can be like the elephant in the room that no one is prepared to mention. In David's example there was a danger that the interviewer would not bring up his age as it might have been considered ageist. Luckily she did bring it up in terms of his lack of experience.

Certain things are taboo areas of discussion and this can be a problem if you think that they might be issues within the company. For example, you might be a young woman applying for a job in a very macho, male-dominated organisation; or a white man looking for a job in a Chinese restaurant. Your interviewer may not bring up the issue for fear of being branded sexist or racist. But they may also not employ you because of the issue.

If you know that an issue exists, you should prepare the reframe for it – and if the interviewer doesn't bring up then you should. In those two examples above, at some point in the interview you need to be telling the interviewer why it's an advantage to the company for you to do the job whether it's a young woman in a male-dominated company, a white man in a Chinese restaurant or any other issue that may have some impact on your employability.

My general reframe to these sorts of situations is the fact that you're widening the scope and the perspective of the organisation. This will inevitably bring more customers and make more money. If it is more of an internal position and less customer facing then you're creating more perspective and creativity. All you need to do is have an experience that highlights your key skills linked to this reframe.

You can use this same general approach for any holes that you have in your CV. For example, if you have been unemployed for a while, travelling, raising children or have even been in prison. What you need to do is look for the key things that you've developed in that period that would benefit the company. You then just pre-prepare a statement about how this is a huge benefit to the company, link it to a key piece of your experience as an example and you are ready to answer the question.

I will say that there are some situations that are never going to look good in a job hunting scenario, but if you have the reframe ready then at least you are in with a fighting chance. Just make sure you know where the holes are and have the reframes prepared. Also, whilst it may seem counter intuitive, you need to bring them up in the interview if the interviewer doesn't because you don't know whether it might be being held against you but not mentioned.

Sometimes your interviewer needs a verbal slap

In over 15 years' worth of working in this area I have met less than two dozen decent interviewers and most of those I've trained myself. A good interviewer is going to give you an opportunity to shine, they will ask questions in such a way that you can highlight your experiences and demonstrate the kind of results that you can get the company. They should take what you say and match it against the criteria that they have. That is the purpose of the interview. Unfortunately not all interviewers realise this and this can lead to them asking stupid or inappropriate questions.

EGO-DRIVEN QUESTIONS

One incredibly dumb question that seems to come up a lot is, "What is the one question that you would dread being asked in an interview?" or something similar. Obviously if you answer this question directly the next thing that they will do is ask you that question. Interviewers playing ego-driven games like this do deserve a verbal slap.

The only way to answer this question is to throw it back at the interview. For example, "The only question I dread being asked in an interview is a question that is keyed to the interviewer's ego rather than being designed to demonstrate my key skills and abilities and how they can be of benefit to the company, for example... (lead into one of your experiences)"

Ok, you could tidy it up a little to make it less confrontational and it would read more like, "The only question I dread being asked is a question that doesn't allow me to demonstrate my key skills and abilities and how they would benefit the company for example..." But there is a point I want to make here. Just because you are being interviewed does not mean the interviewer can go off into ego trips and fantasy land.

HYPOTHETICALS

Here are a few more questions that don't seem to have any point to them. I call them "hypotheticals" because they ask you to look at things that have not yet happened. Here are a couple of examples:

- How long do you intend to stay with the company?

- Where do you see yourself in five years time?

Some HR people trying to justify their function seem to like these sorts of questions as an indicator of your longevity, loyalty and preparedness to stay in the company. I would treat these sorts of questions with contempt. For example, "The issue is not how long I stay, but how well the company is going to hold out good opportunities to make me want to stay. So long as the company is providing me good value then I will stay and provide my services."

Or, "In the next five years I see myself taking career opportunities commensurate with the way my skills and experiences are developing as well as the opportunities that come up for me. My expectation is, should I choose to join this company, that they will keep providing these opportunities for me."

You might not want to be as adversarial as this so feel free to tone it down a little if you wish. I also want you to recognise the trap that a lot of companies will try and set you about company loyalty. This is a form of enslavement that is sold by companies to their employees as a method of controlling them. The reality is about a free exchange of values, so long as the company provide what you want you should continue providing them what they want. If this exchange of value breaks down from either side you should walk away and find somewhere that will give you what you want for your services. Loyalty should never be raised as an issues in interview.

PAY AND CONDITIONS

Why would you turn up for an interview if you were not given some indication of the pay and conditions? If you find a job advertised and they say something like "excellent salary and bonuses" I would be phoning them to ask for a salary range before going to any interview. You might want to explain to them that unless they give some indication of what they are willing to pay you cannot make a decision as to whether to attend the interview.

If you have put yourself in the position that you are at an interview where you don't know the pay and conditions then unfortunately you are in their hands until they open the discussion. If they ask a question like, "What are your salary expectations?" you can only really answer this with, "I expect to get paid what the job is worth based on using my skill set in doing it." You want them to give you a figure or more likely a range first. This would give you a point to negotiate from, but this needs to be done after you and the company have agreed in principle to work together.

The best solution, though, is never to get into this problem; always find out the pay and conditions before the interview stage.

DISCRIMINATORY QUESTIONS

Just because you're in an interview situation, it does not give your interviewer any right to harass or abuse you. Since you have been following the programme from the beginning you will recognise the fact that attitude is the key to successful job hunting. This also means standing up for your rights if you think the interviewer is being inappropriate.

Unfortunately sexism and racism are alive and well, or at least they are in the UK. This is not to say that there aren't other isms out there that also pop their heads up. If you feel a question is inappropriate you should challenge the interviewer about it. A common one that seems to come up is asking a woman about her marital status and if she intends to have children. The reality is that this has nothing to do with her suitability for the role and should not be part of an interview.

Whilst it would seem that this question is inappropriate, I can see some circumstances where you would have to ask the question. For example if the job required you to work in an environment that was hazardous to pregnant women, like certain types of chemical factory, for example, it would be a good question to ask. This is why I suggest asking the interviewer their intent behind the question before deciding how you will deal with it.

If you are asked a question that you feel is inappropriate, you should not only ask them the intent behind the question but also explain why you are asking, i.e. "I need to ask your purpose behind asking that question because on face value it could be deemed sexist."

If you are satisfied with their answer then obviously just treat it as any other interview question and answer with the general formula. If you are not satisfied with their answer then you need to decide how much of an issue it is. I would not work with any organisation that discriminates. Therefore at the point where I am asked a question of this nature and am not satisfied with their answer, I will explain to them why I'm leaving and then leave. I would encourage you to take the same approach.

Using this system you will find that there are many jobs out there for you to go for. Would you want to work for a company that has inherently discriminatory processes and have started to apply them to you, even before you join the company?

Follow the system, get the results

Many years ago, when I was researching interviews and interview techniques, I found myself in a position where I was sitting in an interview having applied with a fake CV, just about to be asked technical questions that I would have no hope of being able to answer. I was asked by one of the two interviewers why I had applied for the job. To the best of my recollection this is how I answered that question.

"I used a fake CV to apply for the job because I knew on face value you would have rejected my experience. You have asked for a lot of technical experience for a role that is really about people management. The issue isn't technical skills, the issue is about focusing and motivating your team to get a result. Let me demonstrate how I can do that with no technical experience."

Instead of throwing me out they chose to listen. I then gave them several prepared examples of how I would get their team working. They got quite drawn into the conversation because the team that I would be taking over was quite a problem and I was explaining how I would deal with them to get them on track. I spent a fair bit of time reframing my lack of experience and technical skills as a great way of drawing the team in and motivating them. They called me back for second interview a week later and then offered me the job. Obviously I couldn't take it, but I was sorely tempted because it seemed like a great job to have been offered.

I expect you to use your real experiences on your CV. In interview I expect you to use this powerful hypnotic answer formula as well as to redefine questions so they show you in your best potential, and to reframe any holes and weaknesses in your experience or qualifications. You now have the ability to answer any interview question and this should give you the confidence to realise you are now completely bullet-proof in the interview. Just use the system and you'll get some terrific results.

In the next chapter we are going to look at the flip side of the coin and get into your chance to ask questions. This is an incredibly powerful opportunity that many interview chumps really mess up. We are going to use it to get the interviewer comfortable with the idea that you are the best candidate for the role.

Asking Your Interviewer Questions

T raditionally, at the end of an interview your interviewer will ask you if you have any questions for them. This is a great opportunity. This chapter is all about the various questions you can ask to capitalise on the opportunity. Let's start by talking about the things you shouldn't ask at this point in time.

Questions not to ask at the end of an interview

There is one thing that a lot of interview chumps seem to bring up at the end of an interview which I think is a complete waste and leaves the interviewer with a negative impression; that is pay and conditions.

Think about it from this perspective: you are making a decision on the company and giving them the opportunity to see how useful you are to them. You should not be attending an interview if you don't already know that the job, the pay and the conditions are in the right ball park for you. There is a negotiation to be done to tie down the details and that should be done after the company has offered you the job in principle. Talking about pay and conditions in the interview is inappropriate and certainly at the end of the interview is a waste of an opportunity.

On the same grounds I wouldn't be asking trivial questions about the job or the company. These sorts of things should have been put to rest before the interview or discussed along the way.

Letting the interviewer know that you are making a decision

When doing your research on the company before the interview, look for any problems or issues that they may have had. The sort of thing I'm thinking of is negative publicity, a falling share price, a fall in sales or performance. I would then ask the interviewer about the issue and what plans the company have put into place to recover.

Another range of questions could come from looking at the long-term vision and the shorter term business plans for the company. A whole range of questions can come up from how they are doing along this plan as well as the obstacles in the way and how they intend to deal with them.

Some interviewers get quite uncomfortable about these sorts of questions. Often this is because they don't know the answers. If they are fudging answers then you should challenge them directly and let them know that it's ok for them to find the answers for you and get back to you. Sometimes they will get defensive and ask you why you might be asking these sorts of questions. If they do this, you can tell them straight that you need to make a decision as to whether you want to work for this company or not. In order to do this you have to gauge how the company reacts to the problems that they have and/or their potential for the future.

The reasoning behind these sorts of questions is to really reinforce the view with the interviewer that this is a two-sided conversation and there are choices to be made on both sides. Right the way through the interview you have had covert control and you have allowed the interviewer to have an illusion of control. This is the point where you let them know that you have been in charge throughout.

It is also an opportunity to show off your knowledge of the company and the research you have done.

If the issue about the company values has come up during the interview then this is a great opportunity to make your interviewer squirm a little. A typical question along this line might be, "What are your personal views about the company values and how do you demonstrate them?"

I would only ask personal questions of the interviewer if I've built up great rapport with them over the course of the interview. These types of questions can be very threatening to an interviewer, so use them with care. The intent behind these questions is to open up a level discussion about company values and how important they are and just to reiterate the point that you care enough about the job to have done research on this level.

The return of future pacing

We have discussed future pacing in a previous chapter and the end of the interview is a great place to plant some more future pacing questions. Here is a selection:

- "If I were to make a success of the role, how would you see it developing over the next five years?"
- "If I got the role and I was doing a great job what

sort of activities would you see me doing?"

- "What criteria will be used to measure my success in the role?"
- "Can you explain the company/department structure and what my place would be in it?"
- "From our discussion today, how do you see me fitting into the team/department/role?"
- "Based on what you know of me, what sort of contribution can you see me making to the company?"

All of these questions require the interviewer to imagine you in the role to be able to answer the question. Some need more rapport and some are bolder than others so again, you need some judgement as to which questions to use.

The end of the interview is an excellent opportunity. It is the place to make a lasting impression with the interviewer. If you have had a good interview then a couple of questions to make sure the interviewer remembers you (i.e. challenge them and make sure they know you value yourself and are also making a decision on the company) and a couple of future pace questions so they are left remembering you doing a great job (even if it has not happened yet) will seal the deal.

Complications
To The System

R ecruitment and selection are important subjects for companies; there is a lot at stake and many organisations live in fear of employing the wrong people. The result is that there are many ways to select people for a job. This chapter is about dealing with some of these issues. Unfortunately all of them add layers of complexity and in certain cases you may not be able to do anything about them.

Recruitment agencies

To understand the issues and challenges around recruitment agencies we need to understand the way they work. For the recruitment agency, their customer is the person paying the bills, i.e. the companies that are hiring them to find people to employ. When you walk into a recruitment agency in response to a job advertisement, you are just a product that they are selling on.

This is important to understand because it means that a recruitment agency will act in a particular way. Their key responsibility is to get a number of the right sort of candidate in front of their customer, the company. This means they are very unlikely to put you in front of their customer if you do not meet most, if not all, of the job criteria. So if you are looking to switch careers, apply your skills in a different industry or do anything vaguely creative with your career, a recruitment agency is unlikely to be of much use.

Another challenge with recruitment agencies revolves around their secrecy. If people knew which company was hiring they might go to the company direct. This would mean the recruitment agency does not get paid. As a result, recruitment agencies are reluctant to tell you the name of the company until they have decided that they want to put you forward for the job. This causes you a problem because until they do, you cannot research the company properly.

If you build a good relationship with a recruitment agency you may be able to get them to do the research for you and tell you the company values and the sort of things that you need to make a decent application. Certainly at the point where they are putting you forward to the company you should know who it is and you can do your research for the interview.

If you are getting the impression that I don't like recruitment agencies when job hunting then you would be right. Here is the biggest issue, in my opinion, with recruitment agencies. Most of the time when using an agency, an employer will be looking to shortlist a number of candidates otherwise they will not feel that they've had a choice. From the recruitment agency's perspective, they will want to show their customer that they can find several good products to choose from. This means that at the point of interview you will have been lumped with several other people and each one of them will have been highlighted as good for the role. You have effectively had all of your uniqueness taken away from you and will have to work harder in the interview because the agency will have made all the candidates look good.

That said, there are some companies that only recruit through agencies, making them a necessary evil. My suggestion is, if you have to use a recruitment agency you treat them as the employer and go through their processes as if it were a job interview.

Once you are on their books, build a relationship with your specific recruiter and make sure you keep tabs on how much work they are doing at placing you. Remember, a recruiter has potentially hundreds of people that they are trying to place. Your recruiter is only going to place those people that are easy to place or stick in their minds. Maintain contact and build a relationship as well as making sure that they think of you as the ideal person for the type of role that you're going for.

Application forms

Many recruitment agencies and companies use application forms and often won't accept CVs. There are a couple of reasons for this: firstly, it standardises the information; and secondly, it allows them to ask specific questions.

Whilst it is quite irritating, after you've spent a lot of time building a top-notch CV, to then have to fill in an application form, I would let the issue go because there are some great opportunities with application forms.

We can split the type of questions on application forms into two categories. The first is the sort of question that can be answered by cutting and pasting parts of your CV. In this case you answer the question in the same format as you have on your CV, i.e. a brief description and several bullet points of key achievements.

The second type of question on application forms actually look like interview questions. And in this case you answer them with the interview formula that we have discussed in previous chapters. I hope you realise that this is a golden opportunity to write down some perfect answers which include an example, the company values and some benefit or future pace statements at the end.

Profiling, personality tests, psychometrics and medicals

Unfortunately, many companies are starting to use these sorts of things. There is little or nothing you can do since companies make it a condition of employment that you should go through these things. I would suggest that you are open, honest and that you don't try and second-guess any of the tests.

The only real strategy I have to deal with these issues is to see if you can be interviewed before any of these tests are put into place. If you already look like you are perfect for the job it is unlikely that you will be turned down because of a profile.

Panel interviews

You should treat panel interviews in much the same as you would treat a one or two person interview. Remember the first two minutes and going through the big and beaming process. You should do this with each member of the panel in turn when you get into the room. Make sure that you remember their names and their position in the company.

When you are asked a question from a member of the panel, direct your answer to that person but maintain eye contact with the others. This is an odd thing to try and describe, but it is a bit like constantly scanning the whole panel but stopping for a few moments longer on the person who asked the question.

If you have the opportunity, research the panel. This is certainly achievable if you're going for an internal position, or a high-level position for which you will be interviewed by the board of directors, for example. You might practice populating your examples with things that you know are relevant to the panel prior to the interview.

Another thing you can do with panel interviews is prepare questions for each of the panel members. At the appropriate time, normally at the end when they ask if you have any questions for them, you can ask each of the panel members questions that are specifically related to them or their area.

At the end of the interview make sure that you close the interview with each panel member. This will probably mean that you shake each of their hands again and thank them for their time.

Assessment centres

Many companies are now starting to use assessment centres, believing that this will make it easier to work out whether you will be good for the role. There are several different types of activities that we are going to discuss and there are some important things that you need to know about assessment centres. Once you understand how these things work, it is easy to get top marks in any of them.

INDIVIDUAL TASKS

The important thing for individual tasks in an assessment centre is for you to understand the criteria that are being measured. Any company that is using activities as a measurement of your capability to do a job needs to be tracking the specific criteria and how they relate to the job. They also have a duty to tell you what is being measured. If they won't tell you I would be very dubious and deeply suspicious of the selection process.

So let's say that they have told you that they are measuring three skills in this particular activity: your organisational skills, decision-making capability and communication skills. Now that you know what you're being measured against, all you have to do is make sure that those particular skills are at the forefront of whatever you do in the activity.

In this example, imagine that the activity is to read through several reports, decide what to do based on that information and write a written communication to your team based on it. You can probably already make the links between the skills that are being measured and the activity. Any well designed assessment centre task should be this obvious. By knowing which skills are being measured it is easy to decide how to approach the task. Obviously you can only be assessed on what you do, therefore you will need to do something for all three in the time allotted.

If I were doing this task I would make sure that I scanned all of the reports, put them into a relevant order, took notes of all the relevant details connecting them together and demonstrated that I was doing this in a very obvious fashion. I would make sure that there were at least two, if not three, possible options and make it obvious that I was using criteria to decide which one was the one I would go for. And then finally the written communication would have some sort of structure and order to it. If I was running out of time I would make sure that some of each criterion was fulfilled.

PRESENTATIONS

There are two different ways that you might get a presentation as part of an assessment centre. The first is just as part of an activity, for example an activity that involves research, decision-making then presenting that information to a group of people. If this is the case, you treat it as any other individual task and make sure that you focus on the criteria that are being measured.

The other reason you may be given a presentation is

because the company wants to see some of your ideas for the role and/or because presentations are part of the role that you are going for. Normally you are allowed time to prepare, whether it is on the day or you were given the task previously. Make sure that you answer the question that you were given and incorporate all the company values and buzzwords as appropriate. Effectively, you will treat this as a big version of an interview answer. Also, note these are great opportunities to add benefit and future pace statements.

The beginning of the presentation needs to reaffirm the question that you were asked and then you link to the solution that you are giving. This solution is similar to the example that you use for your interview answers. What I mean by this is that you should incorporate the company values and make connections to the benefits to the company.

Presentation skills are a little beyond the scope of this book. If you know you have a presentation to do as part of your assessment centre and you have not presented before, I highly recommend spending a while on the internet or in the library getting some core skills. Even more importantly, practise, preferably in front of some people and, if not, in front of a mirror.

GROUP TASKS

Of all the tasks that you could be asked to do in an assessment centre, group tasks deserve special mention. This is because they involve other people and when you add other people into the mix you get some interesting challenges as well as some interesting opportunities.

We can split group tasks into two different versions. You might get a task such as putting together a structured list from information given to you, creating something, or researching and presenting a solution to a problem. The other sort of group activity that is often used in assessment centres is a group discussion. In either case, the strategy to use is the same.

Everything we've said about assessment centres so far applies to group tasks just as well. A group task is generally used to assess a candidate's communication skills, team working ability and leadership potential. There may be other criteria but those three tend to be the favourites.

Often with group tasks the group will realise that they need to assign specific roles to individuals. Even if they don't do so early on in the task, you should volunteer yourself for a particular role. That role is either time-keeper or note-taker. The best role is time-keeper, but if someone has already taken it then note-taker or record-keeper is a good second. There are two reasons that you are looking at these roles. Firstly, from either role you can covertly take control of the entire group, make sure your voice is heard and look like a terrific facilitator. The added advantage is that on face value these roles don't seem particularly appealing and therefore no one in the group tends to want to do them.

This is how you control the group. If you are not managing to get your voice heard as part of the discussion/task, just find a suitable pause, break into the conversation and let them know how much time they have left and then follow up with your opinion/suggestion. If any individual seems to be hogging the discussion, break in, let them know how much time they have left, make a quick comment and ask someone else their opinion/suggestion.

If you are the note-taker, the process is exactly the same except you're breaking into the conversation to clarify what they have just said for the notes.

Now that you have the basic idea, let's just add a few

hypnotic language patterns to smooth the flow. This is particularly useful in group task situation because it can be quite a bizarre atmosphere. I have seen many candidates completely lose the plot in group tasks. I have watched candidates almost come to blows, thinking that the best way to show their leadership skills is to bully everyone else in the group. Whilst it's fair to say that anyone acting in that kind of way is not going to get the job, it also gives every other candidate in that group the problem of being able to show themselves in their best light. If you can handle situations where certain candidates are obviously bullying or hogging the group attention, you will win lots of points with both the assessors and the other candidates. Here is how to do it.

Remember the entire group has given you permission to but in at any time due to the role that you have within the group. At the point where you think someone has done enough talking, or you have a different opinion or it is just time to redirect the flow of conversation, here is what you do.

After you have butted in and reminded everyone how much time they have left, you use an agreement frame with the last comment made. In simple terms, you agree with any part of the statement that you can. If you agree with nothing, you can still agree that the person made the statement. This might come out as, "I agree you said that and I would add…"

There are various types of agreement frame and here are some of my favourites:

- "I almost agree with you and would add…"
- "I agree you think that and I would add…"
- "I don't quite completely agree with you and I would add…"

There are two things I want you to know about these

phrases. The first is obviously the phrase "I agree". The reason that you are using this is that it takes people off their guard and disarms them which then sets them up for the next part the phrase. If you're unsure of this, there is a little exercise I'd like you to try. The next conversation that you are in, just randomly say, "I agree," as the other person is talking and notice what happens. Then take another conversation and just randomly say, "I disagree". Watch the person talking and notice the difference. I'm sure you will agree that these words have a great effect.

The next part of the phrase is, "and I would add..." The word "and" is absolutely vital. The natural inclination is to use the word "but" or "however". Using either of these words will undo all the good that was done with the agreement frame. These two words tend to delete everything that has gone before. You will have noticed this in your own life. Have you ever had the experience where someone said to you something like, "I like what you did, but..." and then gives you an entire list of everything they didn't like about what you did.

The word "and" joins the two parts of your phrase together. So now you can agree with some parts of the statement that they have made and then connect it to anything you want to say even if it is entirely opposite to their original statement. Here is an extreme example just to prove the point.

Imagine you're in an assessment centre with four other people and you've been set a group discussion about the role of the Nazis in the Second World War. Part way through the discussion one candidate says, "I think the Nazis were a great force for good".

You might respond with something like, "I agree that you might think that and I would add, when you consider the amount of murder, misery and damage that

172

they did, you can see that they were an evil force."

Obviously most of the time you are not expecting to encounter such an extreme example, but it shows how dramatically you can change the original statement. This, though, isn't quite the end of the pattern. If you left it here, the original candidate might come back at you and start developing an argument. This is something that would not be good for them or for you. So the last part of the pattern is to ask a question.

The question you ask is normally an opinion from someone else. This has the effect of taking the conversation away from the original person, refocused in the direction you want it to go in, and then giving it to someone else in the group to carry forward. So in the example above, you would agree that they hold that opinion, add your opinion which may be wildly different and then ask the opinion of someone else in the group.

In this chapter we have had a whistle-stop tour of various complications that can happen to the straight-forward job hunting process. In the final chapter we will look at how you can get jobs without having to apply at all.

A New Model
for Job Hunting

We have reached the final chapter. Having got this far into the book, you will have learnt some sexy tools and you will have recognised that attitude is the key differentiator. As you get more comfortable with the tools and techniques that we have discussed in this book, you will find yourself in a position where you have lots of options as to how you shape your career.

At some point, you might need to recognise that the majority of the best jobs are never advertised. Some are shaped and created by the people who step into those roles. Others are filled from personal networks a long time before they would have been advertised.

Five of six years ago, I was on course about some pretty fancy hypnotic communication techniques. One night I was sitting at the bar of the hotel with a friend who was also on the course. We were just chatting and playing with some of the material that we had been learning. It was pretty exciting stuff and we were both keen to talk to people just to practice our skills and see what we could do with them.

A guy walked into the bar and became the target of our attention. My friend seem to get on with him better than I, so I stepped back a little to watch and listen. It turned out that this guy was from Canada and was in the UK on a round of business trips. He mentioned the fact that his life has been made difficult by some operational issues happening in his factories. In the space of a couple of hours, I watched my friend elicit more details, frame the whole thing as a job and sell himself into the role. Subject to ironing out a few technical issues, my friend had been offered a directorship in a Canadian company in the space of two hours through a completely chance meeting in a hotel bar.

My friend is very highly skilled in the type of hypnotic tools are we talking about, but all of the tools that he used have been included in this book in one way or another. Job hunting is actually just the same as selling. It is sales with you as the product and if you start taking this approach you will find there are also some novel ways to get yourself a new job.

Now that you are developing these skills, you have a responsibility to the companies you work with and to yourself. You should only stay in a position where you are providing good value and are getting a good return for your effort. At the point where the exchange of values is no longer equal, you should be heading off for the next job. At the very least, however happy you are in your role, you might want to consider keeping your CV up-to-date as well as an eye on your industry sector's job market.

This chapter is about tools, tips and techniques that you might want to think about in terms of getting the job before it has even been advertised.

Creating your own job

If you are working in a company that you love, but the job isn't quite right for you, consider the opportunity to tweak the job to make it what you want. I have watched, developed and encouraged many people to do this when I've been working as a manager.

Often people believe that a company's organisational

chart and people's roles within it are fixed in stone. This is very rarely the case and most organisations will bite your arm off for good ideas which are going to progress the company's business. The trick here is to make sure that when you're presenting your ideas, you start off with the benefits to the company.

The trap that most people fall into when wanting to change their role is to start thinking and talking about themselves. The reality is that you need to provide realistic propositions as to how this benefits the organisation first.

As usual, there are some complications. The one I find most often is a whole lot of office politics where the idea might suit the whole company but one department has their noses put out of joint, or a manager somewhere is less keen because their personal empire would be dismantled and that sort of thing. The way around this is to make sure, when you're doing your pitch, that you present to everyone the benefits to each individual. If you want to consider this approach properly, consider investing in a few sales books because what you will be doing is selling in the idea of the new role and you as the ideal person to fill it.

Often the issue isn't about majorly restructuring your job, it is just about getting a few more things to interest you into it. The approach is just the same, but made easier by the fact that the only person who really needs to deal with this your manager. Now that you know how to elicit people's values you might want to do this with your manager and feed those back when you make your pitch.

Speculative job hunting

A number of people that I have coached and trained have tried this to great success. To do this you need to have a good idea of the types of companies you want work for, the role that you want to do and how you can provide massive benefit. Often that massive benefit comes from the fact that you might not have the experience that the role normally demands.

This means that in the covering letter you need to reframe that lack of experience as a huge benefit to the company and ideally provide some sort of evidence that it works. In addition, any transferable skills that you have would make a great difference. Here is an example.

Jason was an engineer with a very highly technical skill set. When employed, he was very highly paid because of these skills. But having either worked for a number of organisations that went bust, or got made redundant, he had also spent a number of months on the dole. Jason had had enough and wanted to find a more secure career.

Jason decided that he would like to have a go at general management. This came about partly because it was something he wanted to try and partly because he needed to get into a career stream that would take him back to the kind of salary he was used to. The only sticking point was the fact that Jason had never had to manage anyone other than himself.

What Jason did have was an analytical mind, experience of developing processes as well as good time- and project-management skills. He put his CV together in ways that I have shown you, using key achievements that highlight these sorts of skills. His covering letter made a big deal of how these skills were invaluable to any manager and how his lack of experience in actually managing a team could be a terrific result. The basic idea was his team wouldn't be filled with the latest fancy, pink and fluffy management techniques but it would all be about down-to-earth, practical and pragmatic skills to get the job done.

Jason also did a huge amount of research on each one of companies that he sent a speculative CV to. He modified his CV for each application, making sure that all of the company values and buzzwords featured prominently in both the CV and the covering letter. His covering letter spoke specifically about challenges in the company and the industry and how he was an ideal person to help them sort it out. Jason also made sure that the CV was sent to a named individual and, for the most part, who would be the person that would eventually become Jason's line manager. In each case he followed this up with a telephone call to that individual, looking to close them on a meeting to discuss how Jason could help them further.

If you think that this is looking like a sales job, you would be absolutely right. Jason spent a lot of time and effort learning some sales skills and applying them to getting the job that he wanted. You might want to recognise that usually sending out speculative CVs is a hit and miss affair because it relies on finding the right person at the right time with the right opportunity. Jason sent out six CVs and got five responses, three meetings (they weren't really interviews) and was offered two jobs. The third company that met with Jason contacted him 18 months later and asked if he was still interested as they had vacancies that they thought he would be ideal for.

Networking and raising your profile

A great way of getting a new job is being head-hunted. Isn't the ideal situation having companies and prospective employers beating a path to your door and begging you to join their company? I'm not sure how often this occurs, and I know few people to whom this has actually happened. In all cases, they were known to the employer to some degree before being approached.

On a personal note, I have been on both sides of this fence. In my early 20s I was working as an engineer in a small contract packers that used to supply a very large corporate operation. Because my role meant liaising with the purchasing department of the large corporation, I got to know them very well. When the corporation chose to expand their own marketing and packaging operations, they virtually demanded that I applied for the job. This was a great move for me and one of my key achievements was to double my salary in less than two years, starting with the move to this large company. Remember they approached me and therefore I already knew I had a big negotiating chip when it came to discussing salary.

At the time I was too young and inexperienced to actually recognise what I was doing, but fortunately it was the right things. I've always been innately curious and just love getting to know what's going on. Also the engineering side of me always wants to fix things. The net result was me building a close relationship with the purchasing department and constantly working on how to make their department and my company work better together. The purchasing department had never worked with a contract supplier that was so keen to problem solve. Their perception of my problem-solving abilities was huge, so when the opportunity occurred several people within the department went to their boss and virtually demanded that I should be offered the position.

Later on in life, on several occasions, I have needed to put a team together. Whenever I have had the opportunity I have brought people who I know can do the job in with me. And on occasion I have had to make offers to entice some away from their current positions. This seems to suggest that networking is an essential part of building your career.

Networking is a large subject with a whole toolkit of techniques and ideas. It is also a little outside the scope of this book so we are only going to touch on some simple and straightforward ideas to network and raise your profile. Again, I would suggest investing in a few books that focus on this key skill.

A part of any professional role requires you to keep yourself updated with new ideas, useful contacts and current thinking in your industry. This gives you every excuse to meet with suppliers, customers and competitors. Within the bounds of what is appropriate to your industry, make sure you arm yourself with a whole bunch of questions to find out more of what's going on in their companies and in the business as a whole.

If you are skilful with your line of questioning you can uncover all sorts of problems that they might be experiencing. By being able to offer ideas and solutions you can often come across as very switched on. This will obviously put you in good standing should vacancies occur or you choose to put in a speculative CV.

This was how it used to work in the olden days, it still works and there are so many new and exciting additions to this approach you can take now. The one I would like to mention, as I've seen it used to great effect, is a website called linkedin.com.

Linkedin.com is a website that combines social,

business and professional networking. It gives you the opportunity to put up your career history, qualifications and you can even upload your CV. Many people just load up their profile with all their work-related stuff and then raise their profile on the network.

They raise their profile through several different channels. On the site you can join various discussions, forums and groups. What you can do is either join or create areas that are related to the type of role that you're after. Stimulating some interesting conversations about your area of expertise will very quickly raise your profile. Another really interesting area of the site is a place where you can ask and/or answer questions. I've seen a few people suddenly get connected to hundreds of people just by asking a couple of provocative questions or giving some really spectacular answers to questions.

Another great aspect of linkedin.com is the fact that the site is geared to help you connect with a variety of people. So if there are people in your industry that you would like to get to, you just need to find some connections to reach them. Imagine a situation where you are targeting a specific managing director of a firm that you would like to work with. You find them on linkedin.com and you notice that they are connected to someone who is part of one of your discussion groups.

You get this person from your discussion group to give you a personal introduction to the MD. Whilst that is underway you modify your profile and upload your CV with all the company's corporate values. Your friends gives you a glowing introduction, you ask a couple of pertinent questions of the MD which get them thinking about the type of role that you want to do. The MD obviously goes and has a look in your profile out of curiosity. Once you have built the relationship to an appropriate level, you ask the MD if you can send in a speculative CV based on the role that you have been discussing. How much better do you think your chances of getting that role are if it is the MD who goes down to their HR Department and recommends that they interview you?

Fortune favours the bold

So that's it, we have come to the end of this chapter and this book. You might notice in the few examples and ideas from this chapter that they all use the skills that you have learned from this book, just in slightly different ways.

You might also start recognising the fact that the foundation and the reason why any of the skills and techniques in this book actually work is because you are bold enough to use them. We spent a long time at the beginning of this book looking at the attitude and the beliefs you need, and the misconceptions that you should dispel to make job hunting easy. If you have these in place everything else will happen almost automatically.

I think it is every person's right to have a rewarding and fulfilling job. I also think it is every person's responsibility to find that job. And when circumstances change and that job is no longer rewarding and fulfilling you also have the right and the responsibility to find the next. I hope that this book has given you a little nudge in this direction and some skills that you can use to make it happen in your life.

About Rintu Basu

As an NLP Training Consultant and Coach Rintu Basu specialises in developing people and businesses to maximise their performance in any area. He has developed strategies and delivered training in many diverse subjects from sales and business development to learning musical instruments and playing winning poker.

Rintu has spent the last 15 years training hard-nosed, practical and often cynical people in communications skills, hypnosis and NLP. Having a pragmatic engineering background as well a broad base of experience in business, he has a unique slant on personal development. Rintu has developed a methodology for taking NLP hypnotic language patterns and using them in real world settings to help people get what they want out of life.

As well as running certified NLP courses and maintaining an exclusive coaching practice, Rintu is delivering persuasion skills courses based on his individual perspective on the use of hypnotic language patterns.

Learn more at: **www.thenlpcompany.com**

also by Rintu Basu and available from
www.bookshaker.com